SACKED!

Why Good People Get Fired and How to Avoid It

SACKED!

Why Good People Get Fired and How to Avoid It

RICHARD GOULD

John Wiley & Sons

NEW YORK · CHICHESTER · BRISBANE · TORONTO · SINGAPORE

Library of Congress Cataloging in Publication Data:

Gould, Richard.
Sacked! why good people get fired and how to
avoid it.

    1. Employees, Dismissal of. I. Title.
HF5549.5.D55G68 1986   650.1'3   86-11123
ISBN 0-471-84404-7

Printed in the United States of America

10 9 8 7 6 5 4 3 2 1

Dedicated to the men and women
who earn their livelihood
by working for a boss

PREFACE

Talented and capable people are fired — even when they have achieved good results. This is substantiated by research and the experience of human resource executives, outplacement counselors, and management recruiters — not to mention the untold thousands who have overcome the setback and moved on in their careers.

This book is intended to help good people see more clearly when and why their jobs may be at risk and be better equipped to deal with the turmoil and confusion that often precede actually being fired. The guiding theme is *realism*: to see things for what they are and to stay in command of one's own destiny.

A cornerstone of the book is the Executive Termination Study: a survey of terminated managers conducted in collaboration with Thomas A. Byrnes, a partner in the management consulting firm of Byrnes Mirtz Morice, Inc. The research was based on a survey questionnaire completed by senior executives in 73 corporations representing diverse industries. They ranged in size from sales of 50 million to over 15 billion; more than half of them were Fortune 500 companies. In addition to the survey, interviews with human resource executives from a sample of these companies provided insights into the events and circumstances surrounding individual terminations.

Chapter One delves into the mystery of who gets fired and why. Conclusions from the Executive Termination Study about when the risk is greatest are instructive. Chapter Two traces the progression of events typically found in situations headed for an eventual termination. In describing the human drama from beginning to end, the focus is on the underlying causes, the danger signs, and insights for effectively coping with potentially hazardous situations.

Chapters Three through Six describe the types of conflicts that account for the firing of people, however capable they may be. Each type is explained through a number of case studies, providing an insider's glimpse at what really happened in clashes between subordinates and their bosses. Out of respect for the people involved, and those who provided the instructive case studies, considerable care has been taken to protect confidentiality by disguising the companies and any other identifying information. In fact, the names of the people involved were not even revealed to the author. The intention is to be helpful, not to do anyone any harm.

Finally, Chapters Seven and Eight deal with action—what can be done to avert the disaster of a termination. Chapter Seven provides practical "how to" advice for people who may be caught in a potentially terminal conflict, as well as those about to enter a risky situation. Then speaking to the boss, Chapter Eight recommends steps management can take to avoid the wasteful firing of valuable talent.

RICHARD GOULD

Weston, Connecticut
July 1986

CONTENTS

Contents

SACKED!

Why Good People Get Fired and How to Avoid It

Chapter One

Success Is Not Enough

Who Is at Risk?

Y ou strive to achieve success each step of the way—
working hard, laying the groundwork for the future,
moving up the ranks. It is inconceivable that someone
with your abilities and results would be let go. This
doesn't happen to winners.

But, somewhere along the line, even the best and the
brightest have their setbacks. In spite of years of impressive progress, laudable accomplishments, and enviable
careers, capable individuals are fired.

Research findings, which will be presented in this
chapter, sound a warning: The good guys are not immune from ending up on the outside looking in. Regardless of ability, performance, and years of dedication—
anyone can be at risk. Even some of today's most successful people were terminated at some point in their
climb to the top.

The odds of any particular individual being fired at
some point in his or her career cannot be predicted.
However, it is certainly a prevalent and widespread phenomenon in American industry. The proliferation of
outplacement firms attests to the large numbers of managers being fired every day. It has been estimated that
outplacement revenues have reached $150 million a year.
Research indicates that executive turnover has been
steadily rising over the years.

Yet, in spite of the fact that termination is an ever-
present risk, people are rarely prepared for it. Steady
upward movement has taught the manager to expect
success. The inconceivable news that one is fired is met
with disbelief and confusion. For some, it is traumatic
and devastating.

People often think they know why a termination has

occurred — but most really don't know. Conflict, confusion, deception, and rumors conspire to hide the true facts. Each person constructs an interpretation of why the termination happened, who was at fault, whether it was justified, and who is next. Personal attitudes, feelings, and expectations are easily woven into an individual's perception. The diversity of conclusions about the same termination is sometimes astonishing.

If it's so difficult to separate myth from reality, how is the successful person, who is pushing hard and working smart, supposed to know how to anticipate termination and effectively deal with the situation? This book was written to help people recognize when trouble may be brewing, see the writing that's not on the wall, and take positive action on their own terms rather than allowing a boss to have total control of their destiny.

WHY ARE FIRINGS SHROUDED IN MYSTERY?

Outer Behavior Belies the Inner Turmoil

The following story gives a glimpse of the mystery and confusion surrounding terminations.

From the moment he entered his manager's office, John Collins knew that something was wrong. In the 18 months that Ed Lowry had been his boss, John had never seen him act so strangely. Usually relaxed, Ed's greeting was stiff. His eyes kept darting about the room, never staying put on any one spot for long — certainly not directly into John's eyes. Finally, skipping by any preliminary chitchat, Ed lunged directly into the matter at hand.

ED: It's not working out. For your sake — and the organization's — it would be best all around if you left the company.

JOHN: What? You mean . . .?

ED: Look, I'll do this in any way that will be easier for you. You're a capable person and you won't have any trouble finding a good job.

JOHN: I should just . . . clear out . . . now?

ED: It's up to you. That's probably best. Easier all around. Avoids embarrassment.

JOHN: What will you tell people?

ED: Don't worry . . . reorganization . . . no longer fit. You'll get good references. We'll help you in any way we can. Sorry it had to happen. It's just one of those things.

John kept his cool: Years of corporate training had taught him not to burn his bridges. He politely thanked Ed for the severance package. Their final meeting, much like their relationship, was over before it started.

Not until John was out of his office did Ed realize how hard he had been gripping the lighter in his clenched fist. Tossing it aside, with a sigh of relief, he thought to himself:

"I'm glad that's over with — I hate firing people! It's such a nasty business, but John gave me no choice. It's not that I wanted to hurt him. I hate this. I wish somebody else would do it. One of these days a firing is going to blow up in my face. It's always a little unnerving . . . but I can't think about that. I've got to run the organization and make sure I've got the right people in place. I shouldn't have put it off so long."

When John was safely back in his own office the rage and anguish erupted: "Who the hell does Ed think he is. I've put in years with this company and he just came on board last year. I should have thrown the damn chair at him. That son of a bitch has some nerve. 'It would be best all around' he says. He didn't even have the damn guts to come right out and fire me.

"Now what do I do? I haven't looked for a job in years. What'll I tell Laura? What do I do about the mortgage? The new car? The kids?

"Yesterday, I was a success. Now I'm a failure. I feel strange — almost light-headed. What am I talking about, I feel awful. My career is ruined. I don't know how to look for a job. Who wants somebody who's been canned? What'll my staff think of me? They must have known. Somebody must have had it in for me. I should have smelled trouble . . . but I'm one of the good guys, not one of those mediocre dumbos who screws up and gets fired. I'm damn good. What went wrong? He never told me why he was firing me.

"I'd better get the hell out of here before I bump into someone. After all these years, all of a sudden I don't belong here."

Termination conversations are invariably polite and respectful, with due consideration given to the implication of one's words and actions. Typically, bosses try to soften the blow. Holding back on communicating their criticism of the individual's failings, managers offer innocuous explanations that explain little. The pain is medicated with reassurances that the person will be better off somewhere else. The boss — and the company — do not want to make an enemy of a former employee.

The human drama triggered by this calamitous event is almost always held in check. The terminated individual does not want to jeopardize references. Corporate survivors are well trained in the art of diplomacy. Polite behavior invariably prevails over the inner turmoil. However, terminations are fraught with emotion and conflict. It is a traumatic event for all parties involved, inciting some combination of fear, anger, insecurity, hatred, jealousy, revenge, depression, pity, and resentment. But almost by mutual agreement, both parties conspire to avoid the urge to unleash destructiveness. There are few comparable events in which surface behavior is the mere tip of such a monstrous iceberg.

Inner Conflict Triggers Self-Deception

Termination can undermine a person's confidence and sense of well-being. Given the strong urge to achieve and be successful, the notion that "only losers are fired" provokes devastating dissonance. Having equated termination with personal failure, the individual is left to struggle with puzzling incongruities.

> *If I'm so good,*
> *why was I fired?*
> *I have been successful:*
> *I am a winner who deserves to succeed.*
> *I have been fired:*
> *I must be a loser who deserves to fail.*
> *I am capable or am I not?*
> *Can I be a winner if I'm a loser?*
> *I was respected by management*
> *And now they want me out.*
> *Who cares what they think*
> *But why don't they want me?*
> *Worthwhile people have important jobs*
> *Since I'm unemployed . . .*
> *If I'm unsinkable*
> *Why am I drowning?*

When an idea threatens what we believe about ourselves, as well as the values on which we have constructed our lives, the mind is capable of protecting itself. We find ways to resolve deeply disturbing contradictions and painful dissonance. Facts can be brought in line with beliefs; conclusions can be stretched ever so adroitly to match events. The human mind has the wonderful capacity to see the world as it wishes. The emotional conflicts of termination open the door for self-deceit. In warding off the emotional pain of termination, the issues become clouded; objectivity and accuracy of recollections are sacrificed. A truth emerges that allows people their self-respect and dignity.

A number of years ago, Katherine Spencer, a high-priced executive, was fired. Management handled the termination carefully, telling the outside world that Spencer chose to leave for a better opportunity. Some years later, Spencer bumped into the personnel manager who had been involved in handling the termination. Spencer talked about her fateful separation from the company, expressing satisfaction in her decision to leave when she did. She seemed to have allowed herself the luxury of forgetting that her departure was not of her own choosing.

This reaction may sound absurd, but it is real. Most people know they were fired and never forget it. However, this example shows how far the mind can go to protect itself. And an individual does not have to be some kind of a "neurotic" to play games with the undesirable details of reality.

It is easy for people to impose their own interpretation on a termination when they have not been told exactly and explicitly why they have been fired — and often they are not told. Managers, guided by some mixture of compassion and fear of retaliation, usually soften the blow. Terminees are thus granted the leeway to project their own image onto the events — and this perception is more readily influenced by inner fears, insecurities, and protective defenses. The individuals are allowed to continue to believe in themselves, though perhaps with some nagging doubts.

Spouse and friends are supportive. To reinforce their companion's self-confidence and allay the doubts, they conspire to dispel the terminee's sense of failure. The boss is branded as the culprit; the subordinate is the victim. The distinction between what really happened and the created reality becomes blurred. The truth is forever clouded.

Causes and Effects Become Indistinguishable

The complexity of the events and emotions surrounding a termination makes it difficult for people to unscramble the available evidence. When the termination takes place, people look back for the events that led to the fateful day. People may focus on the straw that broke the camel's back, but may not appreciate the entire chain of events that caused the load to be unbearable in the first place. Even when someone is terminated for events that happened immediately before the firing, there may have been other contributing factors.

Invariably there will be some evidence of poor performance—even the best aren't perfect. People may recall disagreements and arguments or remember occasions when the boss found fault with the individual. Did the boss lose patience with the person for not getting the job done right or was the dissatisfaction caused by animosity?

Problems in working relationships will also be remembered. Did the individual not have the skills to gain the support of others? Or, having seen the writing on the wall, was the organization joining the boss's bandwagon against the individual?

Performance suffers when events in an organization conspire against a particular person. Was the downfall precipitated by poor results or by conspiring events? Causes are easily confused with effects.

Epilogue: What Ever Happened to John Collins?

John was a strong, resilient person. Before long, he got into gear, renewed old acquaintances, mailed a ton of resumes, and shook the trees every which way until the job offers started to come in.

He was an attractive candidate — a history of accomplishments, fast track, and good references. His new boss never even challenged him when he explained his decision to seek greener pastures. No point in having the new boss wondering what was wrong with him. Besides, who would pay top dollar for damaged merchandise?

The job he accepted paid more than the old one and had good growth prospects. His career moved forward as though the firing never took place. But years later, even after getting himself a better job and moving into the upper echelon of corporate America, John thinks back to the firing with lingering discomfort. He's not really sure what happened to him, what he did wrong,

or what he should have done differently. He is
left with a vague sense of vulnerability.

WHY ARE MANAGER'S FIRED?

In spite of the fact that terminations are prevalent, traumatic, and mysterious, little research has been done to
shed light on the subject. However, the Executive Termination Study described in the preface did uncover
some useful clues as to the why's of executive firings. In
addition to the statistical data of the survey, extensive
interviews were especially valuable in revealing insights
into the events that underlie the fatalities.

Are People Fired for Poor Results?

The Executive Termination Study revealed that only 16
percent of the terminated executives were fired because
of their failure to achieve overall results, that is, poor
performance. These executives had the lowest ratings of
management skills, were considered poor leaders, and
had difficulty getting along with others in the organization. In other words, though in the minority, some fired
executives were considered ineffective and incompetent.

The study also showed that in companies with sales
under $1 billion, more than half the terminations were
attributed to inadequate results. However, in the giant
companies, generating from $1 billion to $15 billion in
sales, only 12 percent were specifically fired for poor
results. This dichotomy should not be surprising. In a
smaller enterprise, an executive can more directly impact results.

Managerial jobs in giant organizations have at most an indirect influence on a company's bottom line. Rarely is one person clearly identified as being singularly responsible for any given measurable outcome. Therefore, in large organizations success—and failure—is determined by factors other than results per se.

✓ Do Good Results Protect People from Risk?

In the Executive Termination Study, 45 percent of the fired managers were rated as having achieved adequate or better results. In other words, almost half of all people fired were producing the desired results. Thus adequate results do not protect executives from being fired.

A division of a multinational corporation was foundering and on the verge of being dissolved. Tom Murphy was hired to build the business. Seven years later, after taking this minimally profitable $15 million business to a lucrative $120 million gold mine, he is let go.

Sandra Gordon was hired to establish a new business. She built the start-up management team, created the product concept, and constructed the prototype facility. Within 18 months, the business was off the ground and all set to run on what proved to be a successful trajectory. However, in the eighteenth month Gordon was ejected.

Ellen Daly was brought in to install a new accounting system for a multibillion dollar corporation. She does so on time and to the full satisfaction of both corporate and division management. A year later her boss informed her that she was out.

For 12 years, Don Torrington was the top personnel executive at TranCorp. Then, after being duly fired, he is out on the street with a resume full of his decade of accomplishments.

Does Capability Make a Difference?

You can be fired for poor results and you can be fired if you have good results. Then what is the difference between the person who is fired and the one who is not?

In a study conducted by the Center for Creative Leadership, "derailed" executives were compared with successful ones. As defined in this study, the derailed executives had been fired; the successful ones had a clear pattern of continued career progress with the same company. There was no evidence that the terminated executives were less capable than the survivors.

As follow-up to the Executive Termination Study, interviews were conducted with third parties involved in terminations. The cases provide real-life anecdotes supporting the contention that capable executives are fired.

The chief executive officer (CEO) of a $30 million corporation hired an executive who appeared to have the potential to become president. Although he subsequently felt compelled to fire this group executive, the CEO has little doubt that this ex-employee has the capability needed to run a major corporation.

A senior planning executive was fired. Top management considered her to be an extremely capable strategic planner; the systems she put in place are still being used to manage the business.

A technical specialist had been serving a valuable role; it was acknowledged that few could match his highly developed skills. After he was fired, it took almost a year to find someone who could fill his shoes.

Have Fired Managers Plateaued?

Lee Iacocca, credited with Ford Motor Corporation's great success — the Mustang — was fired. He resurfaced as Chrysler Corporation's irrefutable savior and few doubt the man's executive capability. It is unquestionably rare for so much publicity to surround an executive's rise and fall and resurrection, but the pattern of rebounding on to a successful track is not at all unusual.

A manufacturing vice-president, identified as a potential successor to the president, was asked to leave. In short order, he found a bigger job with another corporation. Within two years a prestigious enterprise sought him out to serve as CEO. He is credited with dramatically — and successfully — restructuring that enterprise's strategic thrust.

After an impeccable history of producing record earnings in one company, a top executive went on to do the same as the CEO of a multi-billion-dollar corporation. The fact that the job move was involuntary would be difficult for any outsider to comprehend or believe.

Another terminated executive went on to be successful working for a competitor. Her new job was virtually identical to that held by the boss who fired her.

This pattern of going on to bigger and better things is found time and time again by outplacement firms. They find that the backgrounds, track records, and capabilities of their referrals usually allow for successful placements into better jobs — in spite of the fact that they did not have secure jobs from which to bargain with strength. One can only conjecture about the capabilities of these successfully outplaced executives. However, their new bosses certainly placed a higher value on the potential contribution of these executives than did the bosses who fired them.

When Is Success Not Enough?

If performance and capability are not the answers for predicting someone's risk of termination, what is? A prevalent belief is that people are usually fired because they can't get along with their boss. Considering just those terminees who had been producing adequate or better results, most of them (70 percent) were fired because they had problems getting along with other people in the organization. More often than not, the problem was specifically centered in their relationship with their boss.

A closer look at those fired because of a bad relationship with the boss revealed that almost every one of them had achieved adequate or better results. Furthermore, the majority of them were rated as having satisfactory managerial skills, especially in the areas of judgment, leadership, attitude, and communication. A breakdown in the relationship with the boss assumed greater importance than performance or capability.

The Executive Termination Study also indicated that those executives caught in a conflict with the boss, for the most part, were usually not at odds with the prevailing corporate culture, nor were they organizational rebels or misfits. Insubordination was also not their style. The follow-up interviews revealed that they had been reasonably adept at organizational life and survival. However, at some point prior to the termination, there invariably was a deterioration in their relationship with their boss. In the final analysis, with a few exceptions, the difficulty was sharply tied to a clash with one individual in the organization — the boss.

Difficulty in the boss–subordinate relationship contributes to the confusion about why a person was fired. Inadequate performance may not have been evident to others in the company, whereas news of a conflict with the boss spreads like wildfire. The boss–subordinate conflict becomes evident sometimes before the ax falls, though it is rarely clear which came first. When caught in the turmoil of becoming a termination statistic, this distinction is important in planning the next move.

One way or another, the relationship with the boss looms large as a vital consideration. After all, the boss is the primary person to determine if an employee is a problem and if termination should be the solution. The boss has the option to interpret the cause of bad events: Are they the fault of an undesirable subordinate or in spite of the valiant efforts of a favored son? If so much rests on this one relationship, it is vital to understand why and when a fatal relationship is likely to develop and erupt.

When Is the Risk of Termination Dangerously High?

When the Executive Termination Study was first initiated, it was thought that most terminations were the undoing of bad hiring decisions. This hypothesis was demolished by the data: only 12 percent had been terminated within the first two years of being hired.

If bad hires was not the major problem, perhaps the cause was the Peter Principle (i.e., a promotion to a job beyond the individual's competence). Executives fired within two years of a promotion to a new job represented only 22 percent of the terminations.

In all, two-thirds of the terminees had been in the

same job within the same company for three or more years when they were fired. Therefore, the correction of bad decisions in hiring or promoting people does not account for the fate of most of the terminated executives.

The follow-up interviews showed something interesting: In almost every instance, the termination took place within 18 months of the terminee's working for a "new" boss. A new boss is someone who had only recently become the individual's boss. Either the boss had recently been put in over the person or the person had just recently taken a new job under the boss. Thus the critical conclusion: Terminated executives are invariably fired by a new boss.

√This means that an employee's risk potential is at a high peak when working for a new boss. Neither track record, results, capability, nor potential may be sufficient protection when there are problems with a new boss. A new boss means starting all over again, proving what you can do, gaining credibility, re-earning your stripes. If the new relationship doesn't click, then the past — prior successes, dedication, loyalty — is the past.

When considering a job offer from another company, an individual can take the opportunity to test the relationship with the prospective boss — and vice versa. Even a promotional opportunity within the same company usually allows for some testing of the fit beforehand. This option is not available to the person who arrives at work one morning and is introduced to a new boss he never met before. From that day forward, this stranger has the power to shape the employee's destiny.

WHAT CAUSES FATAL CLASHES WITH THE BOSS?

What makes the relationship go bad? What kind of conflicts are likely to prove fatal? Are there early warning signs? Can termination be avoided?

The follow-up interviews for the Executive Termination Study revealed that terminations tended to follow a certain course from the start of the new boss–subordinate relationship to the final break. This almost predictable pattern of events is described in Chapter Two.

Also evident from the interviews was that the fatal clashes resulted from conflicts in four areas:

Incompatible Personalities. Something about their personal makeup—temperament, style, attitudes— causes them to be natural antagonists, blocking their ability to work effectively together. (See Chapter Three.)

Divergent Strategies. These are conflicts over where the business should go and how to get it there. (See Chapter Four.)

Philosophical Differences. These clashes involve subordinates acting contrary to the leader's concept of how people in the organization should be managed. (See Chapter Five.)

Role Conflict. In these cases, subordinates do not fit in with the boss's ideas about the role they should be serving within the organization. (See Chapter Six.)

Chapter Two

Collision Course

The Road to Termination

Each termination is unique in its own right. Since no two human beings are exactly alike, each situation has its own unique circumstances. Who can predict when a new boss will bring success or disaster? Patterns have emerged from the many cases of subordinates who were fired shortly after beginning to work for a new boss.

The unfolding of events brings to mind a dramatic play, with characters following prescribed roles and scripts. When in the midst of a real-life drama, the players are confronted with a whirlwind of diverse forces. It is rarely clear to them exactly how their actions will shape ensuing events. But the objective observer, much like the viewer of a staged drama, may capture the sense that there is more inevitability than unpredictability. Once the drama has been set into motion, it seems as though it will not stop until it has run its natural course.

Let us look at how one might script such a play: the antagonists, the compelling motives, the twists of fate, and, of course, the seeming inevitability of it all. For each scene, there are script instructions explaining how the boss and the subordinate act out their parts. The details that make any situation a unique occurrence are excluded — they are for the reader to provide.

The reader has the audience's advantage of being able to peek into the psyches of the characters: to step back from the action, observe the dynamics, empathize, pass judgment — and then walk out of the theater and leave the drama behind. Hopefully, the reading audience will gain sparks of insight.

COLLISION COURSE

The Setting

The time: today; the place: corporate America.

The Cast of Characters

THE BOSS. He has just started a new job. He is typical of many managers: ambitious, dedicated, hardworking, and true to the basic values of fairness and decency. He has come to this job with a track record of noteworthy accomplishments.

THE SUBORDINATE. He has been a prime contributor in the company, having gained acceptance as a capable individual who is destined for continued success. He shares the new boss's drive to achieve, though their personalities are decidedly different.

Act I, Scene 1: Enter the New Boss

THE BOSS. As the scene opens, you are settling into your office and reflecting on the situation. This new job was a critical career move—a significant jump in responsibility. It gives you great exposure, a nifty compensation package, and a substantial challenge. You are determined to succeed, but realistic. Any new situation has its risks. But your feelings of confidence prevail and you move forward with enthusiasm and delight in the challenge.

It is essential that you understand how all the players see the business and how the organization functions. You're sure that changes will be needed, but at this point your objective is to learn. For the first time, you meet the subordinate — your co-star in this drama. He is a key subordinate, critical to your success. It is imperative that you get to know this person and gain his support.

Your relationship starts with a clean slate. You have an open mind. You are hoping for the best; the mood is upbeat. It is the honeymoon phase.

Hoping to find compatibility, you listen for similarities and search for strengths. His experience and knowledge are encouraging signs. You are impressed by his dedication, loyalty, and desire to do a good job.

At this point, the differences in your styles and personalities seem unimportant. You want this person to be effective and to succeed. He brings an extensive knowledge of the business, the company, and the organization. Being new on the block, you find the continuity especially valuable. The last thing you are thinking about is terminating any of these people.

THE SUBORDINATE. You have been with this company for many years. You are accepted and respected for your success. You are comfortable functioning as an integral part of this company. From all indications, your future is bright and secure.

This is your first meeting with the new boss who has been brought in from the outside. You approach him with a mixture of optimism and skepticism. He represents an opportunity for growth. Yet, his arrival generates twinges of fear, jealousy, and resentment. He also represents a potential risk — who is this person and how might he change your life?

Nonetheless, at the forefront of your mind is optimism and a belief in yourself. You are buoyed by your history of success in this company and the strong support you have always been able to count on from management.

You share the prevailing organizational view that the business is proceeding in the right direction and is not in need of a major overhaul. However, there is always room for improvement, and you are open and hopeful about the kinds of change the new boss might introduce. You proceed with positive expectations, giving the boss the benefit of any doubts and presuming that the new boss will do the same.

During this first meeting, you look for and find common attitudes, values, and beliefs. Evidence of compatibility reinforces your hopes, although you reserve judgment. You downplay the importance of any differences, assuming that they will work themselves out. In the past, differences have always been tolerated and have never stood in the way of success. The new boss just needs time to discover the qualities that have earned the confidence of previous managers.

You are concerned about showing your new boss how good you are. You do not focus on his perspective, aspirations, or apprehensions. By the end of the scene you are comfortable and expect to do well with him.

COMMENTARY. This first scene opens with the boss's first day on a new job. The particular focus is the relationship between the boss and the subordinate. These two strangers test the water with each other, checking the fit and compatibility. As they reveal themselves, they gauge how the other responds and reciprocates.

Every person has his or her own values or unique personal constructs for sizing up people and categorizing them as good or bad. Meeting for the first time, they search for signs — words, tone, movements, gestures — to match against their own constructs. Having unique viewing screens, each interprets the same words, actions, or gestures in a different manner. The manager tests for intellect, the subordinate looks for friendliness and tolerance. Neither of them realizes the extent to which their respective minds are recording different versions of the same scene.

It is in their mutual interest for their relationship to proceed smoothly. They must be able to work together constructively and comfortably. The manager senses an ill-defined feeling of incompatibility that will be filed away. This low key scene ends uneventfully. So it seems.

Act I, Scene 2: Assimilating the Newcomer

THE BOSS. This scene shows you building relationships with the other key people in the organization. You recognize that you are entering a foreign organization with a unique culture. Only by trial and error — acting, reacting, alert to counteraction — can you sort out the organization's rules, norms, values, and beliefs. It is a demanding task.

Your personality and experience shape your ideas about the business and how the organization should function. Sometimes you experience tension and frustration as you match your expectations against the realities you find. Compared with what you know from previous experiences, certain actions seem strange or illogical. Only later will you learn that this was partly due to your having misread their signals; actions meaning little to you were very important to them. And vice versa.

As you discover differences between how things are and how you believe they should be, you try to get the organization to understand and accept your views. This is frustrating and stressful — you want the world to mesh and fit with your ideas.

By the end of the scene satisfactory working relationships have been developed. You have settled into a role that feels right for you. The organization is responsive and supportive.

COMMENTARY. The entry of a new boss is a high-risk event. Therefore, it is important to understand what this person goes through when entering an organization. There are strong forces and pressures that influence whether any given subordinate will survive a new boss's entry and integration within the organization.

When joining a new organization, people experience a form of culture shock: The people in this organizational world do not always respond in ways consistent with their expectations. When living in a foreign country, cultural differences are anticipated. However, values and philosophies are not expected to be drastically different between companies. In fact, each organization is unique. It is not unusual for reality to conflict with expectations. This socialization takes a period of adjustment.

Until the new environment is mastered, the boss will

endure a certain amount of stress and discomfort. The new entrant tries to get the organization to conform to how he or she wants things to be; the organization struggles to get the newcomer to adapt to its ways. Boss or not, the newcomer has to work against the organization's natural resistance to change. While the boss is attempting to redirect the organization, the organization is attempting to assimilate the boss. This tugging and pulling throws the organization into a state of flux. If the clash is severe enough, the new boss or an existing employee may be forced out.

Act I, Scene 3: Incompatibility Emerges

THE BOSS. You have acclimated to the organization. Signs of incompatibility with the subordinate emerge. His ideas about the business may be contrary to yours or his approach to managing people goes against yours. Whatever the incompatibility, you are concerned about the subordinate's effectiveness.

Aside from business issues, you have become uncomfortable with him. He's not your kind of person, even though you cannot put your finger on what bothers you about him. Your discomfort is layered on top of your concern that he may not be the right person for the job.

As you play out this scene, your differences become more apparent, although you and the subordinate do not clash over them. You don't want to cause animosity or destroy important relationships. You are still feeling your way with the organization and formulating your plans for the business.

By the end of this scene you are looking at the subordinate with a critical eye. You know his strengths. Now you are looking for shortcomings. You are becoming more and more concerned about the incompatibility.

THE SUBORDINATE. You are getting more comfortable with your new boss, although you are not sure exactly where you stand with him. It is important that you win him over — he can control the destiny of your career. You look for evidence of compatibility, unconcerned about the differences you discover. You didn't always agree with other bosses and it never got in the way of your success. As the scene draws to a close, you persist in believing that things will work out.

COMMENTARY. Critical differences between the boss and subordinate are now evident. They have incompatible ideas about where the business should go and how to get it there. Unless reconciled, the organization and the business would be in a tug-of-war.

There are also personality differences. These are often at the core of the business differences. An individual's personal qualities strongly influence how he or she construes the business and makes decisions.

Whatever the basic nature of their incompatibility, the boss focuses on the issue of performance. However, the boss's conclusions about performance are based heavily on inferences from his interaction with the individual. This leaves a fair amount of leeway for personal feelings to influence the evaluation. Even if the boss goes strictly by hard, measurable results, there is still room for interpretation: Were the results because of the subordinate's actions or in spite of them?

In addition, the boss evaluates the subordinate according to his own point system. This system is based on the constructs and standards the boss considers important. These values may be so self-evident to the boss that he erroneously assumes that everyone shares them. Thus the subordinate is evaluated according to the boss's rules — and the subordinate doesn't know how to keep score, avoid penalties, or win.

As yet there is no observable clash of wills. The players are on the verge of becoming antagonists, but are not in open conflict. Reconciliation is still a real possibility but the honeymoon is over.

Act II, Scene 1: Conflict Irresolution

THE BOSS. A few months have gone by. It is time to begin shaping the organization to suit your design.

As for the executive in question, it has become increasingly evident that this person is incompatible with your expectations. The surfacing of incompatibility has put you and the subordinate in conflict. Your relationship is strained; you don't like dealing with him.

You see some of the incompatibility as simply differences between the two of you — but you consider some of the subordinate's ideas and ways of doing things as being wrong. It's not just that you're the boss. You have both broader experience and a better vantage point for seeing the big picture. Besides, your good judgment has been reinforced through years of success.

While there is no blatant confrontation, you are not passive or silent about your points of disagreement. You aim to be constructive in your criticism, and maintain your attitude of waiting and watching.

Some of your conclusions about the subordinate's capability and performance are based on impressions. Though your thoughts are clear in your mind, you are not sure how easily you could explain or defend your concerns. If the subordinate were to ask you to be specific about exactly what he is doing wrong or what he should do differently, you are not yet sure how you could respond. So you let it ride for now, continuing to observe — but with an even sharper, more critical eye.

As you play out this scene, your growing discomfort is evident, but you stop short of confrontation. You keep an arm's-length relationship; getting too close will only complicate matters.

THE SUBORDINATE. You are still eager and enthusiastic about the new boss, though you begin to realize that the two of you do not always see eye to eye. Certain of his ideas do not make sense to you. You do not understand how he could have arrived at his points of view.

You still don't consider this to be a drastic situation. Your differences will work themselves out. Your judgment hasn't failed you yet. It is just a matter of time before the boss appreciates your views and realizes that this company has its own unique circumstances. His prior experiences just don't apply here.

You are not forceful in letting the boss know the full extent of your disagreement for fear of antagonizing him. The thought that you could be fired is unthinkable.

COMMENTARY. The boss is concerned about the subordinate's ability to meet his expectations. Since his earlier nebulous concerns were not put out on the table, the dissatisfaction has been allowed to fester and grow. He focuses on performance as the primary issue, although his judgment is influenced by various other dimensions of their incompatibility. The subordinate recognizes their differences, but believes that his accomplishments will overshadow any difficulties in their relationship.

The subordinate is in a goldfish bowl with the manager watching his every move. The manager believes that the subordinate knows about his dissatisfaction, but the subordinate is not getting constructive feedback.

Each for his own reasons has avoided open confrontation. While they are both disturbed by their conflict, they do not work at reconciling their differences. Instead, they find reasons to avoid each other—leaving less opportunity for them to come to grips with their differences. As the drama unfolds, the boss and subordinate are becoming antagonists.

Act II, Scene 2: The Boss Struggles

THE BOSS. You have been in this new job for almost a year. You know where you are headed. It has become apparent that the subordinate is not well suited for your plans. An inner struggle ensues.

Until now your part has been straightforward—a rational business executive, thinking issues through in a logical, objective manner. Now you are involved in a conflict over your feelings and ethical principles.

You pride yourself on being able to get the best from

people. The subordinate works hard and does his best —
a sincere, decent human being. He has been with the
company a long time. Given his track record, he can't be
all bad. It will be a personal failure if you can't make it
work. This predicament is a real disappointment — frustrating and irritating.

Although others may not realize it, your compassion
is stirred. At some level, you question your right to hurt
or harm another human being, deprive him of his livelihood, and rob him of his pride and sense of worth. In
the final analysis, firing someone is a hostile act.

Yet business and life must go on; you have a job to
do and a responsibility to the organization, your superiors, and the shareholders. You can't afford to allow
yourself to be dragged down by someone who is not carrying his weight. Besides, if this isn't the right job for
him, he is better off starting fresh somewhere else. You
cannot shirk your duties. Difficult chores come with the
territory.

As the struggle ensues, the frustration grows. The
subordinate has become an irritant — the differences you
had ignored have become annoying. You believe you
have retained your objectivity, but in reality you are sensitive to any sign of a flaw and unforgiving of imperfections.

Your moral struggle does not go on forever. You endure these inner conflicts for a while and then they start
to sort themselves out. The reasons for rejecting this
person gain prominence while the countervailing forces
have become less compelling, irrelevant, unimportant.
The faults are more evident; his strengths have less re-

deeming value. Your survival starts to take priority over his. It becomes more evident that the problem is his fault; you have tried your best to help him but he refuses to change for the better. He takes on the aura of a loser.

THE SUBORDINATE. It is beginning to be evident to you that something is wrong. Your relationship with the boss has become uncomfortable—something is preventing an open and relaxed relationship. You're not getting to know him the way you knew previous managers. You have a nagging feeling that there is something he's not telling you. You are never sure what is on his mind or why he responds the way he does.

An ill-defined sense of insecurity is aroused. It is incomprehensible that your position could be in jeopardy, but things don't add up right and you don't know what to believe. If you weren't so sure of yourself, you'd be very nervous. You must go on as though nothing was wrong—working hard, doing your best, confident that any difficulties will work themselves out.

To complicate matters, the boss is beginning to irritate you. He listens, but is less open to accepting your ideas. Differences of opinion are more evident, though you don't get into any arguments. You are still hopeful and go on as though nothing was wrong.

COMMENTARY. During this scene, the boss struggles with frustration, compassion, blame, and ethics. This portrayal is in sharp contrast to the popular stereotype of the business executive: the tough-minded individual in singular pursuit of money and power, undaunted by moral convictions or compassion. Most managers experience some or all elements of the struggle portrayed in this scene.

As the situation ferments, the boss's vague discomfort grows into justifiable action. In the struggle, the boss's mind is a strong ally. The mind is a wondrous machine that can help people deal with incongruity, dissonance, and ambiguity. Fuzzy areas of gray are neatly resolved into sharp black and white conclusions.

The boss's struggle is served well by these devices. As his dissatisfaction casts a dark shadow over the individual, redeeming qualities fade away and negatives stand out in clear relief. It also becomes easier to logically connect the negatives to job performance. This, in turn, leads to the expectation that the shortcomings will stand in the way of effective performance.

Psychological mechanisms also assist in dealing with the fundamental question in the ethical struggle: Who is responsible for the problem? The attribution of blame is elusive. It is easy to play tag with blame and assign causality to suit our theories. How is one to prove or disprove that poor business results were caused by the executive—or that good fortune occurred in spite of him?

As evidence of poor performance stacks up against the subordinate, the ethical issues become less troublesome. Ambiguity is replaced by consistency. From his perspective, the boss has come to clearly understand the problem and his responsibility. He is free to take full command and chart a direct course of action.

As the clouds begin to clear for the boss, the subordinate's world gets fuzzy. The assumption that all is well starts to crumble, but he's not sure why.

Act II, Scene 3: Communication Deteriorates

THE BOSS. You are still working through the struggle portrayed in the previous scene. It has become evident to you that performance is the problem. You know you must do something about it. Any nuance that verifies the subordinate's shortcomings is readily picked up by your radar. On the other hand, the subordinate's attempts to demonstrate his worth are not accorded much attention.

You let the subordinate know when you find fault with something he has done or when you disagree with his thinking. After all, it wouldn't be fair to fire him if you haven't told him where he is going wrong. However, you stop short of telling the subordinate that you are contemplating his dismissal. His growing discomfort is evident to you, though you do not bring it up. You continue to avoid a confrontation that could force you to act prematurely.

You concentrate on immediate business matters only and don't reach out to build a personal relationship. A safe, arm's-length distance is upheld. Meetings are kept short, casual conversations are avoided, and you don't have much patience for his lengthy explanations. It is harder to fit him into your busy schedule—sometimes you have to cancel his appointments or keep him waiting. Your impatience is attributable to something other than your dissatisfaction with him.

You don't lose sight of the strong feelings that are kept in check. If you play this part correctly, the discrepancy between your overt behavior and your inner reactions should only be noticeable to the most astute observer.

In short, this scene is a good test of your acting ability. If you are well seasoned in keeping your feelings from interfering with business affairs, then this role is fairly easy.

THE SUBORDINATE. Your relationship with the boss is uncomfortable, although you're not sure why. You are not consciously aware of his inner struggle over your future, but some level of your being is picking up on this and is sending you a red alert. The trouble is that you don't know how to interpret the signal.

Your boss is an enigma to you. You see evidence of dissatisfaction, yet there are encouraging signs. The boss has become less accessible, though he continues to treat you with respect. If you accept the situation at face value, you shouldn't be worried. You're not sure what to believe. Your self-concept is thrown out of kilter, vacillating between strong self-confidence and low self-esteem. Your usual pride and self-confidence keeps winning out, but not easily.

The thought even crosses your mind that the boss is contemplating your dismissal — but you can't fathom the unthinkable. You don't dare ask the question: there is no point is giving him any ideas.

The realization of your incredible dependency on your boss grates on you. You have always thought in terms of building a career — a future — with this company. Now you are painfully aware how this single individual can change everything. You can be great, but if he doesn't think so — does it matter? You even get angry with yourself for caring what he thinks of you — but it's hard to keep from wanting the boss's recognition.

In your own mind you become critical of the boss. You question whether he has taken the time to really understand the business or whether he is as capable as he is supposed to be. But you can't afford to blow up — which is all the more frustrating.

Your pent up anger seeks expression and finds its way out. Without your realizing it, there is the slightest undertone in your voice. You are impatient with the boss's explanations and quick to see the flaws in his thinking.

This is a difficult time for you; confusion and apprehension come and go. You are not getting clear signals. You feel like you are in trouble, but can't believe it. You don't know what to do or whom to turn to. It is getting harder to concentrate on your work, but you do your best.

COMMENTARY. The downward spiral gains momentum in this scene. There is no semblance of rapport, closeness, or trust — the relationship is in a state of emotional divorce. Since their worst fears and anger are not revealed, neither fully realizes that their antagonism is mutual.

The interaction between the manager and subordinate is loaded with miscommunication. Each looks for evidence to support what they want to believe and imposes conflicting interpretations on the same events. The boss knows that they are at the threshold of no return; the subordinate has yet to figure this out.

The subordinate struggles to keep his pride and dignity intact. The boss's reactions persist in raising doubts. The seeds of the loser syndrome are sown.

The vicious cycle gains its own momentum. Faulty communication increases the boss's and subordinate's sense of incompatibility and further diminishes their ability to understand each other. The boss's vision gains consistency and clarity; the subordinate becomes more confused. The conflict is coming to a head.

Act III, Scene 1: The Point of No Return

THE BOSS. You have made up your mind: You are going to fire this employee. Everything he does confirms your conviction. The situation is getting worse instead of better. You tried to make it work; he did it to himself. You have no cause to feel guilty and are prepared to take the drastic act of last resort.

Your relationship with the subordinate has reached rock bottom. Your interaction is at its lowest ebb — it is as though you have mentally removed him from the organization. You start asking other people to do things normally within the subordinate's purview. You work directly with his staff without going through him. You allow others to pass your messages on to him, avoiding any unnecessary interaction with him.

Though you have not informed the organization at large of your intentions, you prepare them for the shock. It is important to avoid negative fallout. It will be easier if the reasons for the termination are evident to the organization. This leads you, perhaps unconsciously, to publicly express your discontent.

Given his tenure you want your management's support for your decision to terminate him. If the individual is considered a valued asset, your capability could be called to question. You try to eliminate any resistance to your plan as you build your case. You do not want to find your hands tied when you are ready to make your move.

You are convinced that nothing can save the situation, but maybe a good Dutch uncle talk with the subordinate will help. Your relationship is too far gone for you to attempt the reconciliation, so you call in help from a third party—another executive who has a good relationship with the subordinate. Your last resort comes back with the unsurprising bad news—the subordinate is intractable: he doesn't or won't understand. You are reassured that you have done everything in your power to make this situation right. The time has come.

THE SUBORDINATE. It still seems pointless to confront the manager about your future. Fear and insecurity hold you back; the thought of bringing up this subject is out of the question. Instinct tells you that it would not be a wise course of action.

You continue to work hard at your job, but things do not go as smoothly as they used to. It is difficult to please the boss; he is never enthusiastic about your work. You are not comfortable being with him. He is polite, but not really friendly. He makes you feel awkward and tense. When you work with him, you are not as clear thinking or creative as usual. Your performance in his presence is not up to par.

It has also become difficult to get cooperation from others in the organization—even your own staff. No one refuses to do things for you; you're just not getting the same responsiveness that you have learned to expect over the years. People used to get right back to you; now it takes a while. You feel as though you are being treated like a second-class citizen — a stranger in your own land.

The turn of events is confusing; you're not sure what is happening to you or what to do about it. You don't know whether it is something you are doing or if it is something that is happening to you. It is like being caught inside a pinball machine, being bounced around, out of control. You struggle against an impending sense of insecurity while you forge ahead with confidence that you will not fail.

COMMENTARY. The vicious downward spiral has stabilized. What started as vague suspicions have grown into clear-cut conclusions about the subordinate's effectiveness. The boss, and now others in the organization, have come to expect the subordinate to behave in a certain way. These expectations have an uncanny way of influencing subsequent human events.

The organization is informed, directly or indirectly, that the subordinate is becoming an outsider. People find the boss receptive to complaints about the subordinate. Their comments confirm the boss's convictions and give him the comfort of organizational support. As this mutually reinforcing pattern evolves, the organization withholds the tolerance or forgiveness afforded members in good stead. The subordinate becomes a scapegoat for problems. The ranks close against him.

Although the subordinate's staff have always supported and respected him, he has become a lame duck; the forces that used to compel them to toe his mark are no longer there. His staff is uncomfortable about the turn of events, but don't know how to tell him.

One by one, people join the boss's chorus. Any isolated singing in favor of the subordinate is drowned out. The subordinate struggles to hold on to his own rhythm. Eventually, the unspoken lyrics penetrate—"you're a loser."

The situation becomes increasingly impossible. The hole is now so deep that it is virtually impossible for the subordinate to climb out. The organizational and psychological forces conspire to lock things in their place. This is the point of no return.

Act III, Scene 2: The Ax Falls

THE BOSS. It is now the time to tell the subordinate the bad news. Surgery is never painless, but you will try to minimize the hurt. As you are about to call him into your office, you experience the inevitable apprehension about how the person will handle the crushing blow. But you proceed—it's not the first, and won't be the last. You ask him into your office. It is over before you know it. Once you tell him that he has to leave, there is little else to be said beyond trite apologies and inane comments.

As always, you find that it takes few words to accomplish the deed. In spite of the frustration, you are not a vindictive person. You try to let him off as easy as possible. There is no point in berating him with your displeasure or making a last ditch effort to get him to understand the errors of his ways. An innocuous—"it just didn't work out"—does the job.

Aside from your sense of decency, pragmatics dictate that an amicable separation is best. The organization will be watching with great interest how you handle the terminee. The effect on morale could have its toll. There is also no point in pushing the terminee into seeking retribution and dragging the company into a nasty lawsuit. You have your reputation as well as the company's to consider. Besides, it's a small world and you never know where this person will end up. You attempt to close out the relationship in a decent manner.

THE SUBORDINATE. When the boss asks to see you in his office, something tells you that this is going to be the end. Within moments, your worst fears are realized.

You find it strange that you're not really surprised, yet it is an awful shock. You're not even sure what you are experiencing at the time. Only later does the amorphous feeling sort itself out as resentment, bitterness, and doubt. It is a· shattering experience. Your survival instincts, along with your pride, keep you from showing signs of distress or weakness. You reciprocate his tone of decency and act as though your dignity were intact. You leave his office and stand alone on the darkened stage. A single overhead spotlight accentuates your estrangement — alone in the world during this moment of defeat.

You can't figure out what went wrong or who is to blame. The manager never explained. You don't know what to believe. You can't figure out what you should have done differently. You've never had cause to doubt your ability, but you feel like a loser. The sense of worthlessness won't go away.

Round and round you go, struggling to hold on to your self-respect, bouncing blame back and forth between you and the boss. You have never felt so low or hated so deeply. There is momentary relief that at least these past months of confusion and agony are over. Then, confounded by the questions and contradictions spinning in your head, you walk off into the darkened space as the final curtain falls.

COMMENTARY. An impartial observer might have difficulty believing that the subordinate could not see it coming — all the signals pointed in that direction. The boss believes that he had done his part in forewarning the subordinate, but the message never got through. Unfortunately, the boss never told the subordinate in clear and uncertain terms that he was in danger of being fired. No one set out to deceive the subordinate, but, in a manner of speaking, there was deception.

Outwardly, the fired person takes the bad news well. Polite congeniality is reciprocated. While feelings are brewing beneath the surface, they outdo the British in being polite and honorable to the end.

After the termination, the subordinate is in no frame of mind to sort out the realities of his situation. He can't separate cause from effect. Eventually the subordinate will figure out what happened and why, constructing a reality to suit his sense of self. Deep down he may never be sure; lingering doubts refuse to go away.

Chapter Three

More Than Meets the Eye

The Dynamics of a Personality Clash

S omeone is fired and you are told: "The usual problem — a personality clash." The precise nature of the
conflict is vague. The clarifications you hear are equally
amorphous:

Bad chemistry

Never got along

Couldn't see eye to eye

Rubbed the boss the wrong way

Got on each other's nerves

Didn't speak the same language

These responses offer little insight to someone seeking to learn from the experiences of others. What do
those words actually mean? Why couldn't the boss and
subordinate get along? What rubbed the boss the wrong
way? What triggered the bad feelings? Why couldn't they
understand each other?

Every person is unique, set apart from all others by
a unique bundle of needs, motives, ideas, experiences,
attitudes, and values. Each struggles with life in a unique
fashion against an unreplicable combination of circumstances.

When two such beings are joined together, there is
an infinite variety of ways and reasons for them to react
differently to identical circumstances. Each might pause
to wonder what could be going on inside the head of the
other.

Most personality clashes — both in and out of the
business world — are driven by a mismatch. Some aspect

of one person's personality is at odds with the other's. There are basic differences in the way they think, construe events, and react emotionally. This interferes with their ability to function effectively together.

The case studies in this chapter explore pairs of human beings whose lives crossed, clashed, and then went their separate ways. In each case the people have fundamental differences in how they approach life. The way they experience situations is so different that they have difficulty comprehending or accepting how the other person functions. As is evident from the case studies, the parties to the conflict may not clearly see the dynamics of their clash, but an observer can readily understand and even predict the conflict.

One Saves What the Other Spends

Jack Kotter and Carl Chambers have achieved a high level of success. By any measure, it would be very hard to say that either of these hard-hitting executives have advanced further than the other—position, power, money, and prestige are on equal levels. The similarities do not end there. Over 20 years ago, both started their careers as trainees with Reed Corporation. Their paths did not cross again until a few years ago when Chambers became Kotter's boss—and subsequently fired him.

When asked why things came apart, the company's human resource officer's first reply was "politics." However, as the story unfolded, it became evident that, as usual, it was not that simple.

Chambers rose up in the organization through operations; Kotter had a marketing orientation. Chambers historically contributed to profits through cost control; Kotter made it by increasing sales. Each was well suited to their chosen strategy.

Chambers was a tough, demanding commander, intolerant of waste and inefficiency. He was quick to cut the fat, as though any excess was a despised enemy. Budget wasn't simply a target, but was to be beaten with dogged determination as though life itself was at stake.

Whether it was his money or the company's, he just wasn't a big spender. Never comfortable with anything lavish, he had a natural disdain for any unnecessary frills or fancy extras. His home was as sparse as any operation under his control. Even when he spoke there were no wasted words — direct, to the point, and devoid of emotion.

In the other corner, we find Kotter in his exotic sports car and designer clothing. He was a fun-loving person: wide-eyed, easy smile, and jovial sense of humor. Kotter earned money so he could spend it.

Kotter's progressive mentality produced some

of the company's most innovative new products. His mind was creative and not weighed down with bothersome details. He made inroads into some of the most difficult European markets by using risky and expensive advertising.

Chambers was the president of the Colt Division, headquartered in New York. Kotter worked for him as the European regional manager. When Kotter was based overseas, there was no evidence of friction between the two men. Chambers left Kotter alone to run the region. Then, Chambers was promoted and he put Kotter in charge of the entire division. Things changed when Kotter returned to the United States and moved into an office right next door to Chambers.

From the beginning, Chambers found fault with Kotter's plans and proposals. Being right next door, it was easy to stay close to the day-to-day handling of the business. The more time they spent together, the more Chambers became disturbed by Kotter's ideas. When separated by the Atlantic, Chambers felt compelled to let Kotter run free. Now they were both in home territory and Chambers knew exactly how Kotter should do his job.

The chasm between their personal styles impinged on all aspects of running the business. Pennywise to one was pound foolish to the other. Kotter gravitated toward the unusual, the lavish, the risky; Chambers wanted the safe bets, continuity, practicality. Creative ideas were countered by demands for detailed plans. Enthusiasm was chilled by cold logic. Order was imposed on free flow.

When they disagreed, which was often, Kotter pushed hard for his point of view. But, in the end, however vehemently they might have argued, Kotter knew who was the boss. Once the decision was made, Kotter carried it out. As Chambers continued to impose his will, Kotter's discretion diminished to nothing. With his authority undermined, Kotter was losing credibility as a leader.

Kotter had always enjoyed the support of top management. Before he could be terminated, Chambers had to demonstrate that Kotter was the wrong man for the job. After two tortuous years, management finally gave in and Kotter was fired.

It should be noted that the Colt Division had consistently produced gains in profit for the past 15 years. The results were just as good under Kotter's stewardship as they had been when Chambers was president of the division. As measured by the proverbial bottom line, Jack sustained the same performance achieved by his boss and the predecessors before him.

Today, Kotter is every bit as successful as the

manager who fired him. Looking back, Kotter cannot fully fathom why he fell from favor.

DIAGNOSING INCOMPATIBILITY

Personality differences can create a deep chasm between people. The mismatch can be complicated by a combination of factors and dynamics. Those caught in the conflicts are not always able to step back far enough to clearly see why there was a clash. Only the rare individual can rise above a tension provoking situation and see—with objectivity and clarity—how and why a relationship was self-destructive.

A boss–subordinate clash over personality incompatibility arises when the differences manifest themselves in the work setting. There are four spheres of job functioning in which personality differences can be most troublesome to a boss–subordinate relationship:

How they approach their work—their particular style of planning, organizing, and controlling tasks.

How they think through a problem—the specific way in which their minds seek, sort, and process information.

How they arrive at decisions—the information required, the tolerance for risk, and the flexibility for change.

How they approach other people—their management style.

It is useful to look at how personality incompatibilities arise in each of these spheres and the particular clues for identifying a potential clash. The following is intended to guide the person seeking to diagnose a boss–subordinate relationship that may be in trouble. Both parties should explore how they are matched in each sphere to identify possible incompatibility and a mismatch doomed to failure. The same principles can be used by people deciding whether to join forces.

WORKING STYLES THAT CAN CLASH

A basic aspect of a person's working style is how he or she plans and organizes tasks. At one extreme is the "cautious planner" who carefully spells out each and every step before making any move. With a sharp eye for what can go wrong, all contingencies are covered. Everything must be in its proper place—neat, orderly, and structured. The consummate bureaucrat. Slow and cautious wins the race.

The natural antagonist to this type of working style is the free and easy "fast mover" who weaves and dodges without a plan. Inspired by an idea, the fast mover is ready to go into action. Detailed plans and tight structures are stifling and constraining—merely excuses for inaction.

The cautious planner can't conceive of starting out without a map; the fast mover won't be confined by one. While one fights to control randomness, unpredictability, and disorder, the other is intolerant of a neatly ordered, structured world. One is fearful that the impulsive, seat of the pants style is bound to end in disaster; the other is concerned that they'll be buried in the details and never move forward. In the final analysis, speed is the simplest clue: the slow planner contrasted with the fast mover.

Control is another aspect of a person's working style — the energy and attention devoted to ensuring that things happen a certain way.

At one extreme is the "tight controller" — a staunch administrator with frequent checkpoints. The tight controller is constantly looking back at the plan, the targets, and the timetable. There is little freedom to move outside the lines. Rules and policies are to be followed with religious fervor. Administrative perfection driven by control.

Then there are the "free spirits" who move with freedom and flexibility. They won't be constrained by rules or structure and have little patience for either bureaucrats or autocrats. They delegate easily. Subordinates are given wide latitude for movement — "just tell me when you're in trouble."

One writes voluminous policy and procedure manuals; the other ignores the rules. Carefully worded memoranda emanate from one; brief hand-written notes from the other. The tight controller always knows the status of every project while the free spirit is out looking for new ground to cover. The neatness of their offices — especially desk tops — is a good clue to these contrasting types.

A controlling manager sees the free spirit as irresponsible, unpredictable, and undisciplined. He never knows when the subordinate will deviate from the established order. The freer subordinate may rebel against such a manager, fighting the efforts to constrain him or her. In the struggle for freedom, the free spirit may not keep the manager fully informed — an intolerable state of affairs for a controller. The natural response is to tighten control!

A free-spirited manager is frustrated by a subordinate who is always concerned about having rules and standards. From this manager's perspective, constant checking destroys initiative, stifles creativity, discourages risk taking, and slows down progress.

A conflict in work style was apparent in the clash between Jack Kotter and Carl Chambers at Reed Corporation, where order was imposed on free flow — a controlling manager did not take kindly to the inspirations of the free-spirited subordinate. Consider the situation at Graystone Industries where a subordinate's loose work style clashed with a model of order and stability. This case, seen through the eyes of a third party, shows how one can spot the clues to incompatibility.

The Stolid Pillar and the Free Spirit

A management consultant is called in to help a chief executive officer (CEO) sort out a disturbing conflict. This expert — a Sherlock Holmes in the science of understanding the art of human relations — was created to provide an incisive look at two real-life personalities in conflict. The detective will tell the story in his own words.

Yesterday I received an urgent call from Charles Bain, the head of Graystone Industries. It is now early the next morning and I'm waiting in his reception area. His secretary, a prim and proper elderly woman, asked me to be comfortable outside his office. Wasting no time, she immediately went back to her work.

I've never met Charles Bain, but I did have some background information. He had a strict Midwest upbringing. In high school he was a model student and citizen. College waited until after he served his country during World War II. Having graduated with honors from a top engineering school, he went to work at Graystone's testing laboratory. A meticulous individual with a penchant for detail, he was a master technician. To this day he is known for having instituted the company's intricate quality control procedures.

Working long and hard, he steadily climbed the ladder, a rung at a time, to top management. He has a reputation for building strong loyalty — a fair, evenhanded leader whose word is his bond. Following the example of his deeply rooted work ethic, the headquarters is imbued with the aura of his seriousness.

At our appointed meeting time, not a moment later, I was ushered into his office. Considering his lofty position, the office was plain and ordinary. Instead of the usual artwork, the walls were lined with numerous service awards. A remarkably clean desk with everything in its place — a sense of order. Even the massive policy and procedure manuals, well worn from use, were neatly lined up on their own shelf.

He was a sturdy figure of a man who obviously took good care of his physical well-being. He greeted me with a firm handshake, his reserve ever apparent. Wasting neither words nor time, he got right down to the matter at hand.

Four months ago Bain completed a long drawn out search for a group president. He disliked bringing outsiders into the organization, commenting how "they rarely fit in the way we do things around here." He carefully scrutinized every candidate, including the prime finalist — Ellen Miller.

Bain had explored every aspect of Miller's experience and credentials. Bain did not learn much about the candidate's personality, but he sure knew exactly what had been accomplished, as well as when and how. The candidate's experience was a perfect match for the job.

Continuing in his logical, matter-of-fact style, Bain explained his concerns about Miller's performance. "When Miller describes her plans for the business, I can't follow her logic. I try to listen carefully, but she jumps all over the place with her ideas. She acts like she knows what she's talking about — but she loses me. I never know what she'll think of next — she's so flighty and unpredictable.

"I can't get her to write her ideas on paper; maybe she really hasn't thought them through. I can't pin her down. She always wants to change things; I wish she was more practical. She doesn't know enough about the history of the company and isn't experienced in the way we do things. It's so easy to see why her ideas won't work."

As I listened, an odd picture was emerging. Miller sounded incompetent — illogical, flighty, impractical, out of control. But she had a superb background and track record. What could have sent her off the deep end? How could she have made it this far and be this bad?

After a thoughtful pause, Bain went on: "You have got to help straighten out this problem. Maybe I'm doing something wrong. I will do whatever is necessary to get this worked out. That is my obligation, but I don't even know where to begin."

Having said his piece, he glanced at his watch. Our 45-minute meeting was over — right on schedule. I was whisked away to Miller's office at the other end of the building. It was apparent that most of the employees fit the mold — serious, industrious, conservative. The place was almost somber with the absence of even occasional chitchat or laughter. Activities proceeded at a steady pace. The workday was totally devoted to work.

Apparently Miller had arrived at her office just before I did. She was busy getting geared up for the day. The moment she spotted me, she popped right up from her chair and greeted me with a friendly smile and a warm handshake. She treated me like a long-lost friend.

Her office was furnished identically to all the others, but in sharp contrast to their neatly organized appearance, hers looked like she was doing 17 things at once. This alone was probably enough to unnerve her compulsive cohorts.

We chatted over coffee before getting down to business. After a few minutes of getting comfortable with each other, I proceeded with my assigned task. She was open to my involvement since she knew full well that she was having trouble with her boss.

She quickly took me through her background, skipping over the details, only touching the high points. Her brief overview provided a good sense of her accomplishments and the thrust of her career.

Readily at home with colorful language and vivid metaphors, her story was both fascinating and impressive. She couldn't wait to finish talking about her past and proceeded to spend more time on where she was going than where she had been. She was full of ideas: an expansive imagination coupled with an untiring optimism. Wherever she turned, she saw the upside potential, never the pitfalls. She had no trouble visualizing where the business could go.

I could easily see why Bain, a cautious individual dedicated to cold, hard facts, would feel uncomfortable with this upbeat, imaginative, and expansive person. It would be impossible for Bain to accept Miller's visions for the future at face value.

Thus the consultant came to realize why the subordinate was not destined to succeed with this boss. A more compatible manager would value Miller's innovative ideas, with not a single doubt about the logic or practicality of her thinking. The loose style, cluttered desk and all, would be taken as positive signs of movement and flexibility.

A reconciliation of their disparate styles was not achieved and Miller was asked to leave. In searching for a replacement, the consultant advised Bain to look beyond the technical qualifications to test personal fit; it takes a certain kind of individual to fit his style of working. Miller was able to understand why she was a bad fit and would consider this in picking a better match the next time. The consultant hoped to sensitize both of them to the little things that could mean a lot — like whether the next person they hook up with sees the glass as half empty or half full.

THINKING STYLES THAT CLASH

Although all minds operate in accordance with the same basic neurological principles, there is wide variance in how different people approach problems, what kind of information they seek, and how they analyze what they find. When certain people scan their environment and their memories for relevant information, they focus strictly on concrete, physical facts that can be seen, touched, and measured. For them, past experience is the only teacher. They aptly fill the role of corporate historians.

Their opposites gravitate to ideas and images. They are willing to imagine the possibilities and speculate on the future. For them, the past experience does not dictate the future. They are willing to rely on intuition and hunches. They are futurists, not historians.

A manager who demands hard facts sees a futurist's "speculations" as impractical. Conversely, an expansive thinker will be frustrated by a subordinate who is stuck in the past. The historian's views are rejected for being uninspired and too narrow. Either mismatch will result in a skeptical boss and a frustrated subordinate.

Another dimension of thinking style has the concrete thinker at odds with the conceptualizer. The concrete thinker focuses on the details you can see and touch. The conceptualizer deals in images and abstract concepts. They seek patterns and overlook the specific details. While they see the similarities between disparate events, the concrete thinker is discerning the differences.

A concrete thinker finds it difficult to follow the logic of a subordinate's ideas that are not grounded in specific details. Without clearly visible connections from one point to the next, the thinking appears illogical. The subordinate is considered impractical and full of ideas that don't make sense. Conversely, the conceptual manager easily loses patience with a subordinate who can't follow his or her train of thought without constant explanations.

Whichever side the boss is on, differences in thinking style can lead to deep misunderstandings, difficult commuication, and an impasse to gaining agreement on ideas. This is evident in the following case study of an intuitive thinker who despised being contradicted by an analytically minded subordinate.

Cold Logic Defies a Politician's Instincts

After nine years with a big eight accounting firm, Susan Parness went to Charter Medical Supplies — a division of a diversified conglomerate. Over the next 10 years Charter's sales went from $5 million to $50 million and Parness had risen to controller. In keeping with her strong work ethic, Parness was dedicated to her job. Being blessed with a superior business sense, she contributed greatly to Charter's decade of success and had been rewarded accordingly. Parness was even identified as a contender for the presidency, competing with the top marketing executive, Michelle Sherwood, who had been at Charter for three years. In spite of this competition, Parness and Sherwood made it their business to work well together.

Sherwood's claim to fame was her astute marketing judgment. She was an instinctive marketer, adopting strategies that felt right. To her, market research was a lot of statistical mumbo jumbo used by people who didn't have the intuition to sense the mood of the marketplace. Besides, she knew that people could use statistics to prove either side of an argument. She was paid good money to make judgments, and so she did.

Sherwood was a master politician—Machiavelli would have been proud. Sherwood understood power: who had it, what they wanted, and how to gain favor. She also valued loyalty and harmony. She was uncomfortable when people disagreed. Thus she strove to keep people placated, to be liked by her superiors, and to keep peace in the organization. Some people considered Sherwood a manipulator: a smooth talker who bent with the political winds.

For someone like Sherwood, the ideal subordinate aimed to please the boss. She especially liked subordinates who understood that the name of the game is to elevate their manager in the eyes of her superiors. In the same vein, she had little tolerance for anyone second guessing her thinking. To find fault with her ideas was to find fault with her.

Parness came from a different school of thought. Her approach was perfectly suited to financial work. She did not embrace an idea until she saw clear-cut measurable evidence leading to the conclusion. Parness insisted on being able to follow the step-by-step logic of an argument. The idea that something was correct because it felt right did not compute in her mind. She accepted nothing on instinct alone—preferring to dig into the facts until an idea fell or rose on logical evidence.

Parness's focus was on the validity of ideas, not feelings about the person who has the ideas. The management at Charter was cut from a similar mold: relationships were never shattered because someone disagreed with your ideas. Nobody was punished for finding fault with someone else's thinking. At least not until Sherwood made it to the top.

Parness saw nothing wrong with commenting on a flaw in someone's logic—even in the presence of that person's boss. Because Sherwood was quick to see others as being politically motivated, she interpreted Parness's behavior with great suspicion. In fact, Parness was politically naive and did not tune into the politics of relationships. Since she did not think in those terms, she was oblivious to Sherwood's political perspective. She knew that Sherwood would do anything to please the boss, but never realized the extent to which Sherwood considered politics as an end in itself.

So here we have two capable executives: both intelligent, energetic, ambitious, and pragmatic in their own way. They had the capacity to be an invaluable complement to each other; careful analytical thinking as a counterbalance to instinct. But their clash prevented them from taking advantage of the other's strengths.

Once the power was granted to disengage the relationship and be rid of an uncontrollable threat, it was done. Within six months of being promoted to the presidency, Sherwood fired her foe.

Was a power struggle at the root of this clash? Was the real problem a manager's insecurity? Were the boss's negative attitudes and expectations influenced by the intensive competition for the presidency? Notwithstanding these issues, the differences in their styles was an essential ingredient to the clash and the fatal ending.

DECISION-MAKING STYLES THAT CLASH

Differences in how people think are reflected in their decisions. The conclusions of one may be based on factual, measurable, irrefutable proof, while another relies on visions and concepts. Personality also comes into play, especially with regard to decisiveness and flexibility.

Decisiveness — how fast a person makes decisions — ranges from excruciatingly slow to extremely rapid. Consider the situation when a tentative individual is matched with an impatient, quick-draw, impulsive type. Undoubtedly, they would drive each other to distraction. While some indecisive people may be happy to find someone willing to make decisions for them, they are generally frightened by unharnessed impulsiveness. For them, making decisions without careful forethought is irresponsible and dangerous. Conversely, the fast-moving individual doesn't hesitate to make a choice and move on it. For some, quick thinking is a sign of strength. It is not unusual for them to go forward and not wait for the cautious to catch up with their thinking.

If you find yourself frequently becoming impatient with a boss's slowness in deciding issues, ask yourself whether he or she finds you too impulsive. Does the manager let you act on your judgments? Are you sent back for more study? If you think your boss jumps to conclusions too quickly, he may consider you indecisive. Does your manager give you a chance to finish your analysis? Does your manager jump in with the answer?

Chambers at Reed Corporation and Bain at Graystone were both relatively cautious. They carefully studied the issues before making decisions, and invariably took the safer, more conservative route. They had something else in common: frustration with subordinates who, from their perspective, made decisions without carefully evaluating the facts or the risks, throwing caution to the wind.

The other aspect of decision making is flexibility.

Even after making a decision, flexible managers are willing to change their minds. Rigid managers never bend. Regardless of how quickly a decision was arrived at, flexible people maintain an open mind to new information. If they discover that their assumptions are faulty, they begin the decision-making process anew. In an indecisive person, the slightest hint of contradiction reignites the vacillation.

At the rigid or inflexible end of the spectrum are those who treat decisions with great finality. These people get settled into a groove and strongly resist any attempt to change their position. Contradictory evidence is greeted with annoyance and possibly even distrust.

The flexible manager has little tolerance for such resistance to change; a rigid subordinate is a roadblock to rational decision making. When such a boss meets an unbending force, the frustration and anger are usually mutual. The boss may become infuriated with a subordinate who won't yield. Even the most stubborn subordinate will recognize a dangerous impasse — although the subordinate may not stop to consider that a fatal countdown has been triggered.

A rigid manager could view a flexible subordinate as being wishy-washy, lacking conviction, or just plain weak. If a subordinate feels that his boss is too stubborn, the subordinate should be alert to the possibility that the boss considers him too bendable. On discovering such an incompatibility, the flexible subordinate may find a way to adapt and avoid a fatal clash. In contrast, the rigid of heart, by nature, doesn't readily adjust to new discoveries.

The Zen Master Faces the Fastest Gun in the West

Self-confidence comes in many forms. There are those who have the outer bravado of strong words and quick action, but not David Fielding. His confidence is built on a foundation of inner peace: he has come to accept himself as he is, foibles and all. This wasn't always true, especially during the early years of his tough climb to the top of the heap. But life has been good to him: His career has fallen into place; his family is a joy; and his health couldn't be better.

Fielding's temperament and outlook have shaped the way he manages an organization. He can patiently allow nature to take its course: "Let's first see how things fall into place — don't move precipitously." But this tolerance for ambiguity should not be mistaken for indecisiveness or complacency. Rest assured that he knows what he wants and persists in getting it — he didn't rise to the stewardship of a major corporation by lying back while life passed him by.

Ross Shore has yet to experience the same inner peace. Even when sitting still, he seems like a body in motion: tightly coiled tension ready to spring into action. There is no greater devil for him than an unresolved issue. Matters have to be decided quickly and closed with definitiveness.

Having a brilliant mind, he is able to quickly

take hold of even the most complex question. Moreover, getting to answers before most people, Shore feels that it is a waste of time to go around gathering the ideas of others.

Shore was remarkably talented at organizing the disorganized, providing clear-cut structure for getting things done. Nothing flopped around in the wind when he was in charge: every duck was lined up, each task specified and assigned. The job got done exactly as planned.

Imagine these two individuals as equal partners of a business. Depending on how they dealt with their differences, this could be a useful complement. Fielding was hoping this would happen. An astute executive, he recognized that his open-ended style did not create a strong sense of discipline in the organization. He felt that it was time to bring someone like Shore into the management group. This concept was superb — in theory.

Shore's task was to put a sophisticated planning process into place. Throughout his career, he had been successful in highly structured environments and had become a master of operational controls.

Fielding stood back and allowed Shore to install the management systems. In the course of helping managers with the process, Shore became intimately knowledgeable in the nitty-gritty of the operations. In fact, he became more familiar with the day-to-day details than his boss.

Fielding started turning to Shore for input on decisions impacting the business operation. Shore had good judgment and brought different perspectives to the party. Fielding was astonished with the speed at which Shore would mentally take hold of a situation, sort out the pros and cons, and bang out a clear-cut, unequivocal answer. While Shore had a knack at being right most of the time, Fielding's natural instincts dictated that life could not always be as simple as Shore made it seem. As time went on, new constructs emerged in Fielding's mental image of Shore: impetuous, overconfident, cocky. Shore had become a puzzle: "How could such a highly disciplined, detail-oriented professional be as impulsive as he seemed?"

The discomfort became even more serious when Fielding started to bump into Shore's inflexibility. Shore was not all that stubborn, but the relevant reference point is the boss's Zen-like flexibility. Fielding keeps an open mind, always receptive to other people's thoughts. He also likes to give himself a chance to digest the ramifications of major decisions. This drove Jack up the wall.

Neither of these individuals represented the far extremes of thick-headed rigidity or wishy-washy indecisiveness. However, from where each of them sat, those derogatory constructs came to fit how they saw each other.

In spite of their differences, Fielding was

getting what he wanted from Shore. Managers were more disciplined in their planning; follow-up was vastly improved. Shore remained a frustrating puzzle whose ideas continued to be worth soliciting. Fielding could have accepted this situation, but Shore became increasingly persistent in imposing his unequivocal thinking on division managers.

Though Shore was finally done in by his persistent battles with field management, incompatibility with the boss was an essential ingredient of the fall. The conflict of styles had nudged Shore's risk quotient close to the danger zone, making it easy for subsequent events to pull him over the red line. A less tolerant boss would have fired Shore long before the organizational uprising.

LEADERSHIP STYLES THAT CLASH

Personality makeup is a key determinant of a person's management style. There are as many approaches to leadership as there are different personalities. However, certain extreme styles, when mismatched, have notable potential for producing antagonistic relationships. Consider pairing any of these four types of leaders:

Forceful Drivers. Forceful drivers demand rather than request and focus on results, not feelings. They are direct and autocratic in their dealings with others. Their single-minded drive to take charge supersedes concern for human frailty; they are indifferent to inner feelings.

Friendly Diplomats. Friendly diplomats are people-oriented: personable, warm, and comfortable. A high value is placed on building close, supportive, and mutually satisfying relationships. Interpersonal conflicts are avoided. Guided by naturally sympathetic human instincts, friendly diplomats are easy to get along with. They rely more on the ability to conciliate than on the authority of their position.

Enthusiastic Persuaders. Enthusiastic persuaders lead with excitement—firing up the troops to charge up the hill. They have undaunted confidence. Quick to see the opportunities in a situation and seemingly oblivious to the risks of failure, enthusiastic managers set an inspiring tone for people to follow. Words of encouragement and approval are freely offered. Their enthusiasm is contagious.

Objective Analysts. Objective analysts yield to reason not emotion. Feelings are out of place in rational business matters—the mind not the heart should rule. They lead by logic, expecting people to follow the superior solution. They listen to ideas; teach rather than tell people what to do. Letting others take the initiative, objective analysts readily delegate.

A driving manager may see an amiable subordinate as being too soft. The bluntness of a forceful leader may be harsh and painful for a sensitive subordinate. Dissatisfied with such softness, a hard-nosed, demanding manager may push even harder. This, in turn, increases the tension, deepens the wounds, and causes the hurt subordinate to withdraw. The gap between them widens and the conflict escalates.

An analytical person may find the emotion of someone enthusiastic to be excessive and out of place. He is uncomfortable with the excitable person who seems so out of control. Conversely, an enthusiastic person sees the cool responding analyst as lacking a sense of urgency. Looking for things to move fast, the careful analyst is too methodical and lacking the emotional spark needed to be a good leader.

At Graystone Industries, Bain managed in a logical matter-of-fact style; Miller sought to rally support through enthusiasm. The analytically minded manager is not inspired by a subordinate's undaunted spirit.

Sherwood at Charter Medical Supplies was a classic diplomat—a first class politician. Parness was virtually oblivious to political considerations. While her boss was concerned about how others would respond to an idea, she focused only on its logic and verifiability. This proved fatal.

The chasm between Fielding the Zen master and his quick-thinking subordinate was widened by differences in their compassion toward others. Fielding found that Shore was too anxious to control and never stopped to listen to people. The following case describes a parallel situation involving an amiable executive who hired a no-nonsense manager.

A Sharp Rock Strikes a Soft Heart

Edward Williams and Nick Diamond had much in common: both grew up in New England, graduated from the same alma mater, and devoted their careers to the same industry. Though Williams was older by 14 years, they shared the same deep abiding work ethic and dedication to the bottom line. So Williams, the plant manager, was pleased when Diamond was hired to manage the production department. Personal qualities aside, Diamond had the expertise needed to fix their troubled facility.

Williams is a congenial individual. He is comfortable to work with and easy to get to know. He cares about people and takes great pride in his efforts to be of value to others. He is in touch with his own feelings and readily senses the concerns of others. He is naturally attentive to the good in people.

Diamond focuses on business results: getting things done. He is a direct and forceful manager who expects to be heeded. He speaks his mind, freely correcting people or challenging their ideas. Williams found Diamond to be cold and distant. Conversely, from Diamond's perspective, Williams worries too much about people's feelings when the business should come first.

During the initial job interview, Williams sensed that Diamond did not have a strong people orientation. Diamond kept the interview conversation sharply focused on business. This was a reasonable thing for a candidate to do, so Williams did not read anything into this early sign of their disparate temperaments. Since these initial discussions did not veer outside the straight and narrow, there was little opportunity to sample the candidate's depth of compassion or any other personal feelings. Diamond remained calm, cool, and collected — a bit reserved for Williams' taste. But they had a common view of the industry and were in full agreement on what was needed to save the floundering operations.

As time went by, the differences in their emotional makeup began to surface. Williams found his new employee a bit dull, emotionally flat, lacking a sense of inner excitement. In the same vein, Diamond sometimes felt embarrassed when the top executive freely expressed personal feelings. He saw this as a weakness. Diamond became even more guarded with his own emotions when they were together. Thus tension began to seep into their relationship.

This was only one dimension of the problem. Diamond was matter of fact when challenging anyone's ideas — even the boss's. Williams was unaccustomed to being treated with such abruptness, but he could live with this. However, it hurt him to see other people being treated so thoughtlessly. He could not understand how someone could be so insensitive.

If Williams was not so sensitive, much of Diamond's social behavior would have gone unnoticed. Many managers would see his bluntness as a virtue. When Williams put himself in the other person's shoes, he may have been more sensitive to Diamond's remarks than the person who was actually on the receiving end. Nonetheless, the forceful subordinate clashed with the amiable boss.

A FINAL COMMENT ON CLASHING PERSONALITIES

It is critical to understand how your personality fits in with the boss's. Do you complement or clash with his mode of functioning? To start with, you must "know thyself." Understand the style and manner in which you work, think, decide, and lead. Then do the same assessment for your current or prospective boss. Put yourself in your manager's shoes; imagine how the world might look to him. If you had your manager's temperament and style, how might you react to someone with your traits? The relevant measuring stick is the boss's point of view.

An important clue is the boss's reactions to different people, especially decisions. Who is rewarded and promoted: the tougher, results-oriented managers or those with a more patient, tolerant attitude? Are you uncomfortable with how your boss handles people who make errors or miss targets? If you were in your boss's shoes, would you have made decidedly different decisions about the people?

In your role as boss, it can be useful to understand

why you don't get along with certain subordinates. At the very least, before hiring someone, take the time to get to know more about the fabric of the person and how he or she is likely to fit in with you over time. Therefore the best precaution for avoiding a hiring mistake is to test the fit and heed your instinctive reaction to the candidate. Keep in mind that the candidate's experience, knowledge, and skills are only part of the picture.

Just because a boss and subordinate have drastically different emotional styles doesn't always mean the end is near. An emotional boss may value an unflappable subordinate who provides the check and balance of objectivity and reason. The perpetually calm boss may recognize the importance of managers who can bring spirit and excitement to an organization. The value placed on such complementary personalities may go unspoken — it is a rare boss who acknowledges imperfection or dependency. The wise subordinate learns to recognize opportunities to bring unique value to the relationship without forcing a clash.

It is clear that personality has a major influence on how people work, think, decide, and lead. This can be taken one step further. Personality is often a critical factor in determining the strategic direction chosen by executives, their philosophy of managing an organization, or the role expected of key people. Thus a boss and subordinate with personality differences may also find they cannot get on a common track about business strategy, management philosophy, or organizational role. Serious conflicts in these three areas can undermine a working relationship and result in termination. These issues are explored in Chapters Four, Five, and Six.

Chapter Four

Whose Dream Is This Anyway?

Irreconcilable Strategies for Success

A business strategy is a vision of where a business can go and how to get there—the formula for success. The boss's vision is the guiding light for setting the direction of an organization. When the leader has a crystal clear vision and is firmly committed to his dream, there may be little tolerance to forces attempting to divert the business off this track. Besides, a train can't go in two directions at once. If the boss is convinced that you are going in the wrong direction—departing from his vision—something has to give.

The following cases show various kinds of strategic issues that can underlie critical differences between a boss and subordinate. In all instances, the parties to the conflict were intelligent, capable, and rational businesspeople. Why should there be such drastic differences in their thinking? Wasn't there any way for them to be reconciled?

Let's Go for Broke

Charles Kheel is a successful business executive. Though he never had the stomach to go into business for himself, he did well serving the role of entrepreneur within the security of a large corporation. For eight years he was president of Clarity Limited, a subsidiary of a billion-dollar public company. During this time the business grew and prospered. Top management viewed him as an astute businessman who exercised reasoned judgment. He was an amiable, easygoing individual who worked well in the corporate structure. Although he didn't have a burning desire to break any world records, he enjoyed the fruits of his labors and was dedicated to building his financial worth.

Clarity manufactures sophisticated high fidelity speakers, catering strictly to the discerning audiophile. In following this strategy, they captured a profitable share of this narrow market segment without going head to head against the big name brands. Given the results, the parent company left him alone to pursue this steady course.

Enter Joanne Locke, hired to be group executive of the corporation's consumer electronic divisions. Locke was a woman in a hurry to reach the top; she was out to make a big name for herself and to do it fast. She was a brilliant strategic thinker, able to see business possibilities beyond the vision of most executives. Her ambition drove her to keep looking for a golden opportunity.

After a brief indoctrination in the business, Locke had plotted a new master plan for Clarity's future: to become the leading producer of electronic audio equipment. Unlike Kheel, she hungered for a healthy chunk of this massive and lucrative market. The driving wedge would be a stepped-up product development effort, supported by a huge advertising campaign. The price of entry was not going to be cheap, but it could catapult Clarity into the major leagues almost overnight. The risk was high; the payoff incredible. This suited Locke's vision of herself. She was determined to become known as the woman who built a formidable force in the home electronics industry.

Inevitably, Locke and Kheel clashed. Each was firmly convinced that their conception of the business was best for the long-term health of the company. Kheel was afraid that they would not survive against the giants; Locke could not fathom ignoring this fertile field. Kheel was distressed at Locke's insistence; Locke was losing patience with her subordinate's resistance. The organization suffered through the strife of being torn by two conflicting masters.

Termination finally ended everyone's agony. Faced with an ultimatum from Locke — "It's either him or me" — management felt compelled to support the dependable manager who for years had produced good margins. The clash over strategy had put both executives on the brink of being fired. In the end, the ax could have swung either way.

The leader's job is to set strategy. Newly hired managers face a real crisis when they discover that key subordinates do not share their view of where the business can go and how to get it there. At Clarity the two executives had incompatible views of both the market and the strength of the competition. When two leaders continue to press to move in such incompatible directions, termination may be imminent.

Isn't it possible that neither executive at Clarity was wrong? Couldn't they both have had more of an open mind to each other's ideas? The crux of the problem was that both were intractable in their beliefs — there was no meeting ground to reconcile Kheel's need for stability and Locke's drive for a smashing success.

Intellectual differences of opinion gain emotional momentum as a conflict progresses and positions harden. First the ideas are wrong; eventually it is the person who is no good. The person who disagrees goes from "not fully understanding" the business to "wearing blinders" and eventually becomes "stubborn and stupid." Both parties go through a progressive deterioration in their perception of the other. The wedge driving the antagonists apart is no longer different opinions about strategy.

To Grow or to Cut Back: That Was the Question

Frank Parker was hired by James Elder, the CEO of ChemTech Corporation, to be the group president over three specialized chemical businesses. When Parker assumed command, the profits of all three divisions ranged from borderline to badly bleeding. Although Parker lacked direct experience with the specific products manufactured by these businesses, he was no stranger to the chemical industry. He was well seasoned as a line executive and had a good track record in managing a variety of businesses.

Based on what Parker learned from his division presidents during his first six months on the job, he was optimistic about the prospects for these businesses. He believed that the secret to getting these businesses back on their feet was the revitalization of sales growth. This would require an immediate infusion of capital and fresh new approaches to product promotion.

Whenever he talked to Elder about his plans for expanding the businesses, he found himself butting a brick wall. Although Elder did not know what should be done to resuscitate the business, he simply could not be convinced that Parker's ideas for increasing sales would work.

Their disagreements often evolved into arguments. Decisions about what to do about the business continued to be in flux. Believing that a personality clash was at the root of the problem, ChemTech brought in a professional counselor to help straighten out the faulty communication. When this did not succeed, Elder decided that it would be best if Parker left.

Parker's replacement did not share his predecessor's optimism about the failing businesses. He believed that the only way to remedy the situation was to cut costs to the bone. Overhead and investment spending were sharply slashed. The replacement squeezed minimal but acceptable returns from two of the companies; the only way to stop the drain of cash from the third was divestiture.

Given the healing powers of time and the benefit of hindsight, management gained a better understanding of the conflict between Parker and Elder. Looking back, it was evident that Parker never actually investigated the details of what was happening in the marketplace or the processing plants. He never brought concrete facts to support his proposed strategies. Thus Elder continued to follow his own instincts about the business. Their differences were irreconcilable because neither Parker nor Elder had gotten close enough to the businesses to know the specific facts that could have provided the basis for a meeting of their minds. At the time it wasn't clear why they could not agree; it seemed like they just couldn't get along.

Parker was an incisive thinker and nothing was wrong with his native intelligence or business knowledge. He had been successful in running businesses for other blue chip corporations. Why were things different for him in this situation? Being in highly competitive and relatively mature markets, the management philosophy at ChemTech was to run "lean and mean." Managers were expected to roll up their sleeves and do their own detailed analysis. In the past, Parker always had the luxury of a sizable staff to do the digging. This had enabled Parker to stay focused on the big picture, leaving to others the day-to-day running of the business.

Unfortunately, neither Parker nor Elder realized the extent to which Parker had grown dependent on extensive staff support to do his homework. After moving on to an organization more in keeping with his prior experience, Parker continued along the fast track he had been on before his clash at ChemTech.

In the cases so far, the strategic differences have been from an external, marketing perspective. The conflict can be just as fierce when two managers disagree over internal operating issues — such as the application of new ideas and technology.

Putting a Sharp Knife into Expenses

Bob Lamm was in charge of the back office operations at Craig Securities, a regional brokerage house. Starting as a clerk, and in spite of limited education, he rose to this position in the course of his 23 years with the company. Not only was he a respected member of management, employees at all levels of the operations organization looked up to him as a strong leader. The operation always ran smoothly under his command. This allowed senior management to stay away from the humdrum routine of the paper factory. Even when the firm was acquired by a financial conglomerate, nothing had changed for Lamm. The new management was more interested in bringing in the money and letting the back office take care of itself.

Then it happened. Two years after the takeover, Nancy Pike was hired to oversee the administrative functions, including the back office operations. Unlike any of her predecessors, Pike chose to get her hands dirty and take a close look at this finely tuned operation. Although Lamm was actively involved with his counterparts in other firms and was exposed to current developments in the field, he never applied them in his own shop. Pike felt that it was essential to improve processing efficiency and saw many opportunities to trim operating expenses. Her first priority was to streamline the organization through automation.

Lamm firmly resisted. Pike offered to let him hire consultants to help plan the changes. Lamm would have no part of it. There was a long-standing bond of trust and loyalty between Lamm and his subordinates. This bond served the smoothness of the operation, but kept it locked in antiquated technology.

Pike tried to work with Lamm, but the tug-of-war went on for months. It finally became evident that Lamm would not budge. As long as Lamm was in charge, Pike would be unable to automate the operation. Thus Lamm was fired after many years of valued service—a victim of a clash over operating strategies.

THE RISK OF A STRATEGIC CLASH

More often than not, a clash over strategy occurs when someone from outside a company is imposed over tenured management. This was true in all the cases cited, although the newcomer was not always the survivor. The Executive Termination Study found that most terminated executives had been with their companies for a number of years—only 12 percent were newcomers— fired within two years of entry. Therefore, tenured managers should not be complacent when an incoming new leader wants to take an organization into new directions.

Sometimes a new manager is hired to revamp a tired strategy that is no longer working. The new manager starts out with a mandate to chart a new course and alter the direction of the ship. Unfortunately, he is often confronted with a crew that is skeptical about the new captain's vision of the future. The new captain may have to move quickly to take advantage of the marketing opportunity. If the crew cannot be swayed to support the captain, they may be replaced by mates who are ready and willing to pursue the new course.

WHY CAN'T MANAGERS RECONCILE THEIR STRATEGIC DIFFERENCES?

Does the introduction of new business ideas have to result in terminations? Can't intelligent people faced with the same facts arrive at a common truth? Isn't it self-evident, after reasonable analysis, which strategy is superior? The questions have a ring of naiveté to them, but nonetheless are deserving of answers.

First of all, personality differences between two managers often underlie their pursuit of different strategies. By reputation, managers try to be objective, analytical thinking machines. Alas, they are in fact mere mortals. Managers are not likely to pursue strategies inconsistent with their personal makeup: temperament, motivation, values, attitudes, preferences.

Kheel, the president of Clarity Limited, was comfortable in stable, predictable situations; the thought of gambling for big stakes was enough to keep him awake at night. Locke, on the other hand, was driven to make the big time; it was the front cover of *Fortune* or nothing. Conservative people set conservative targets and gamblers take risks. It is inconceivable that these two executives could come up with one business strategy acceptable to both temperaments.

A manager's strategic ideas are also shaped by his business experience. When a certain strategy has been successful, people have reason to choose that same direction again and again. When a new manager's experiences are substantially different from the other players in the organization, strategic questions are confronted with entirely different assumptions and mind sets. They have learned different truths about what makes the business tick. Their theories about the business can be so different that their words may not mean the same thing to each other.

To Kheel, Clarity Limited was a healthy business; it made sense to keep doing what they were doing well. Locke's background (and ambition) told her that they were ignoring a gold mine if they didn't go for the broad consumer market. One person's concept of good results was failure to the other.

Before coming to Craig Securities, Nancy Pike had seen how computer technology reshaped the speed and efficiency of large clerical operations. It was not a new idea for her; Pike's experience had taught her the kind of efficiencies that could be achieved. Her subordinate, Bob Lamm, had learned that a smoothly running operation was rewarding; it had earned him respect, position, and a comfortable income for many years. The volume of transactions kept growing faster than operating costs. But to Pike, his new boss, this was not an acceptable standard and the old ways had to go.

Finally, the culprit may be conceptual obsolescence: thinking based on outdated knowledge. The world is moving rapidly at an accelerating pace. It is exceedingly difficult for people to fully comprehend the implications of today's cultural changes and technology explosion—yet they impinge directly on the competitiveness of almost any business, even those that are not technology based.

Technology and culture have been moving forward from the past into the future like a rocket. If one manager falls behind another in keeping up with the changing world, they are likely to develop differing notions about where to take a business. The manager who falls behind becomes "conceptually obsolete." The changes in the world have not been integrated into the person's comprehension of the business environment.

This is a warning for managers who do not expose themselves to the many different aspects of our ever-changing world. Unfortunately people tend to believe that they are in touch with reality: Who wants to think that their view of the world is out of date? However, some people's views are obsolete.

If you have been with the same organization for a number of years, do you seek out people beyond the protective walls of your company? Are you in touch with people actively involved with new technology? Avante-garde ideas? Contemporary viewpoints? Do your associates help challenge your concept of what turns people on today? Do they open your eyes to what is happening right now in the marketplace?

SUMMATION

The message of this chapter is: Create the opportunity to challenge your assumptions before a new boss does it for you!

When a recruited executive is injected into an established organization, irreconcilable conflicts over business strategy are most likely to erupt when the new entrant's experiences, ambitions, and temperament represent a major departure from the prevailing norm of the organization. Long-tenured employees are more likely to fall behind than more mobile managers who have been exposed to a variety of situations. The established, stable institution tends to be insulated from the subtle changes taking place outside its bounded cocoon. The tenured person should recognize that a new leader will have a certain way of construing the world—and there may not be much room to accommodate the old ways.

When it is apparent that your strategies don't mesh, try to understand why. How much of the difference is anchored in dissimilarities in your respective experiences and temperament? Are these insurmountable obstacles or is reconciliation possible? If you really believe in your ideas, you have every right to try to prevail. However, if you keep pressing and there is no accommodation to your ideas, you may find yourself on the outside looking in.

Chapter Five

At Odds With the Establishment

Incompatible Management Ideals

M anagement philosophy concerns the ideals by which an organization should be managed. When the head of a company has definite ideas about how the organization should function, a subordinate acting against the grain of these beliefs can be in for a difficult time. When these values have been inculcated into the organization's culture, the battle will more surely bring defeat.

The following cases involve fatal conflicts over management philosophy. The clashes were typically triggered by the entry of a newcomer who is at odds with the entrenched culture of an organization. Casualties of this type of conflict can be the nonconforming newcomer or the career employee who resists the new leader's determination to reform the organization.

Drowned by the New Wave

Cultural change usually evolves over a period of years. Sometimes, with little warning, it hits like a hurricane. In his thirty-fifth year with Home Products Corporation, an unsuspected current caught Ned Marks off guard.

For the past eight years Marks had been the uncontested general manager of the office equipment division. His authority and control of the organization were well established — no one called him Ned. He maintained order and stability with a firm hand. Rigid rules and detailed procedures covered any contingency. His boss had little interest in getting involved in the business, so Marks was left alone to be the ruler of his kingdom. Furthermore, he was located a comfortable distance from the corporate headquarters.

All was smooth and uncomplicated until his boss retired. The replacement, Don Roland, had a mandate to revitalize the company. Within weeks of his arrival, Roland sought to introduce sweeping change in the cultural fabric of the organization. His first step was to attempt to heighten the sense of urgency: Tough performance standards were imposed with a sharp focus on results.

While he brought in a tough mentality, Roland believed in giving people the opportunity to succeed. A strong proponent of decentralized management, he felt that the extreme central control imposed by Marks contributed to their having lost touch with a changing competitive picture. He wanted Marks to break the business into regional profit centers, so that local managers could focus their energy on the particular demands of the different markets.

From Marks's point of view, Roland's ideas were impractical and incredibly naive — they would lose control of the business. Marks had a well-established chain of command. Besides, he felt it would be irresponsible to put the field people who were ill-equipped to handle the responsibility in charge. For Marks, the boss's concept of how to manage the organization just did not make any sense.

Roland believed in giving everyone a fair chance to succeed. During his first full year on the job he had only brought in one key manager from the outside. He hoped to change the culture without replacing the people. He tried to get the existing management to understand his vision of how the company could be revitalized. However, he soon began to lose patience with their unwillingness to break away from the organization's historical beliefs and patterns.

Marks wasn't the only resister. The whole organization had been together in the same groove for such a long time that they reinforced each other's views of the impending changes.

This was a tightly knit family fending off an enemy; the boss's management philosophy was threatening the fabric of the organization. They were right and he was wrong.

Roland didn't have the outward appearance of the stereotypical tough authoritarian leader. While he is drawn to challenges and seeks high achievement, he is patient and understanding in dealing with people. However, his will to have things done his way could take the shape of a steamroller. The organization underestimated the possible consequences of refusing to give his ideas a chance. For as long as anyone could remember, there had been a "cradle to grave" attitude about job security. No one expected to be fired just because they didn't go along with the boss.

Roland tried to work with Marks. When Roland explained his ideas on how to manage the business, Marks listened. But Marks heard only the words that would allow him to keep from changing his ways. They never had a confrontation. Instead of open disagreement with the boss, Marks responded with silent obstinacy — no shouting, no resolution of differences. This frustrated Roland. The resistance began to feel like downright arrogance. The situation became intolerable. Finally, 14 months after he had become Marks's boss, Roland fired him. Marks couldn't believe it — the prior leader would never have done that. Marks was not the only one asked to leave — only the first.

Caught in the Shifting Sands of Decentralization

Argus Industries had experienced strong, healthy growth over the years. Upper management was relatively stable: Most key positions were occupied by executives who had put in many years under the same CEO. Historically, division presidents had only limited authority to make decisions; almost any change required corporate approval. Extensive procedures had to be followed for expenditures to be approved; numerous signatures ended up on a request before it became a decision. The division heads grew up with this philosophy—it was how things were done.

This same bureaucratic philosophy existed in the personnel area. Any personnel decision had to flow up the channels to the corporate personnel department: No one could be hired, fired, promoted, or given a raise without layers of approval. Management used the system to contain salary dollars and to force people to think twice before changing anyone. Long-term employees were not easily fired; their loyalty and dedication were respected.

Norma Henderson, the senior vice president, corporate personnel, had the administrative machinery well geared-up to perform this valued function. Her efficient staff understood the rules of the game, which decisions to allow and which to turn down.

Just over the last couple of years, a new breed of manager was brought into the divisions. Compared to their predecessors, these new managers were far more aggressive, decisive, and independent. Most of them came from companies where they were full-bodied decision makers. The restrictive system of approval at Argus was an anathema to these high-powered managers. Being well bred in organization life, they gradually pushed for change—there was no outright rebellion. Top management recognized the incongruity of hiring extremely capable executives without giving them the latitude to exercise their valued judgment. Slowly but surely the division executives gained greater authority. Decentralization began to take hold at Argus.

Henderson worked closely with the division executives to help build the staff they needed to be self-sufficient in handling personnel matters. The divisions were relatively unsophisticated in the personnel area and could benefit from the new ideas that were emerging in the human resource field. One by one, Henderson helped install capable personnel professionals in each division.

Henderson viewed these changes as healthy for the business. However, her day-to-day functioning did not accommodate itself to the new world that she helped create. The historic pattern of control through approvals persisted. Henderson's administrative machinery was clearly out of synch with the prevailing wind of decentralization.

Henderson was caught in a dilemma. She new the transition was appropriate and inevitable. But what would happen if she stopped performing this historic role? How could she hang on to being a valued member of management?

The division executives grew increasingly impatient with this state of affairs. A tug-of-war ensued between the division executives and the corporate staff. When division management became highly vocal in pressing their case, senior corporate management became compelled to fix the problem. This triggered involuntary turnover in the corporate personnel office — starting at the top.

Senior management appreciated Henderson's past contributions, and the decision to fire her was not taken lightly. After all, the transition of letting go was not easy for management either. However, the persistent conflicts were stealing valuable energy and time from key people. Something had to give. After Henderson was terminated, the transition was far from over. When a new personnel officer appeared on the scene, others in the department were replaced. And so the turnover cascaded down into the organization.

When Staff Takes Charge of Line Management

People meeting Jeff Noland at a social gathering usually find him to be an articulate, sophisticated, and witty gentleman with a magnetic memory for interesting facts and details. Noland enjoyed being impressive. He didn't realize that his "superiority" suppressed others into quiet timidness.

Noland had good reason to be proud and self-confident. He had progressed rapidly through the ranks of three blue chip corporations. He became an expert in strategic planning systems and had exerted a strong influence on the management of these businesses.

Kane Corporation had just gone past the billion-dollar mark; it was time to adopt the ways of the big boys. The division heads were good operators, but needed guidance in thinking through the long-term strategies of their businesses. The informal planning was not rigorous enough for the next — more difficult — stages of growth. Also, the company needed to be smarter about how they allocated capital to these cash-hungry businesses. Miles Wagner, the long-time leader of Kane Corporation, hired Noland to put the processes in place.

Top management liked Noland's ideas and knew from the start that he was the right person for the job. Noland had a crystal clear concept of what was needed and how to put the systems into place. When he presented his ideas with a great sense of authority and conviction, the division presidents willingly followed him. There was no resistance to the impending transformation that was taking place in how the company was being managed.

During Noland's first full year on the job, management learned how to use the new tools. In the second year, the programs began to serve an important role in management's review of business operations and investment decisions. By the third year, the systems impinged on all key

business decisions within the operations: bud-
geted expenses, plant construction, purchase
agreements, and sales targets. As the master of
these procedures, Noland began to assume a piv-
otal position in Kane Corporation. Approval for
all key financial decisions had to pass through
his hands.

Noland's authoritarian bent found a natural
avenue for expression. He was not shy about
passing judgment on the submissions crossing his
desk. His opinions were expressed with strong
conviction and left little room for negotiation.
Eventually, his self-confidence was magnified
into arrogance and his beliefs became dogma.
The staff lieutenant had become a marine drill
sergeant. Worst of all, Noland lost any remnant
of sensitivity for the feelings of others.

Managers found that their latitude in running the divisions had slowly withered away.
Since Wagner championed the installation of
these new management processes, the managers
assumed they had to live with the new ground
rules.

Noland's peers at corporate staff had fully
supported the installation of these programs.
Not being sophisticated in these processes, they
weren't sure what they could contribute anyway.
But as the situation unfolded, they found themselves outside the periphery of a very powerful
force. The field managers started to complain:

Who did Noland think he was? What was he up to? The suspicion and distrust were infectious.

The inevitable friction ignited sparks that Wagner could not ignore. His expert planner was destroying the very management philosophy he valued so highly — the ability of division heads to run their own operations. This was a difficult situation for Wagner. In certain areas, Noland was invaluable: His analysis of potential acquisitions was truly impressive; the tracking of internal operations was vastly improved; and capital allocation was on a rational track. Noland had brought to Kane Corporation the very management disciplines Wagner wanted.

Wagner wanted to save the situation. There had to be room for someone with Noland's capabilities, but the strife could not continue. He asked an executive, who had worked closely with Noland, to intervene. This did not change anything. Noland still did not see that he had a problem. Going one step further, Wagner brought in a consulting psychologist. But he could not get through to Noland either.

Noland's authoritarian nature struck directly against the grain of Wagner's management philosophy and the corporate culture at Kane. His strengths no longer outweighed the price that was being paid. The decision to sever finally came.

That's Not How We Treat People Around Here

Certain United States corporations are known for their long-standing emphasis on humanitarian values. This tradition was carried forward through Harrow Company's three generations of family ownership. The family was genuinely concerned about the welfare of employees and the community at large. Over the years, this ideal became the backbone of the corporate culture. Employees reciprocated this trust and had a strong sense of loyalty to the company. The typical employee stays with the company — and plans to enjoy the generous retirement benefits.

Though openings invariably go to someone within the ranks, on rare occasions, when the required technical expertise has not been developed within, an executive is hired from the outside. A new hire at the managerial level has no better than a 50–50 chance of succeeding in their organization. When the outsider is not one of "their kind of people" — regardless of his capability — he is doomed to failure. The organization system rejects those that go against the flow of the culture.

A recent example is the hiring of Brenda Newcomb to manage a troubled division. Being uniquely knowledgeable in the technology essential to the production of an advanced control device, Newcomb was one of those rare exceptions to the rule of promotion from within.

Newcomb earned her reputation in designing computerized controls. The market for these devices was exploding and yet Harrow could not get a respectable share. At the core of the problem was the reliability of the units they were producing. Engine manufacturers were losing confidence and turning to sources with better performance records. Newcomb was knowledgeable in the technology essential to solving this problem.

Newcomb is a woman of action — full of enthusiasm and verve. She walks fast, talks fast, and could almost knock people over with her dramatic physical gestures. When she has a job to do, all this marvelous energy is sharply focused on getting results.

Her middle name is expediency. She can be impatient with organizational formalities, such as having to follow the chain of command. In communicating with people she is also direct and to the point: If she has something to say, she says it. She has little patience for social amenities and chitchat. This would hardly be noticed in most organizations, but the people at Harrow took extra care to avoid hurting someone else's feelings. Though not meaning to be abrasive, Newcomb's brusqueness could take on a sharp edge in such a sensitive environment.

After a year and a half this failing business

was turned around. Incessant difficulties in producing consistent product quality were virtually eliminated. A creative promotion campaign quickly revived customer confidence. Once again the company had a winner and Newcomb was the hero of the day.

Then, during Newcomb's second year, sales and profits flattened. Was this the fault of this exceptional manager who had worked a miracle? Given her past performance, Harrow's management had justifiable confidence in her ability to turn the business around. The team she inherited was ready, willing, and able to support her — but she did not seek their counsel. She felt it was up to her to figure out how to revive this business. It didn't seem to make sense to follow the advice of the people who failed to get results. Newcomb made all the decisions. Things were done her way. The role of her management team was to execute her ideas. However, they resented being excluded from decision making. It was their deep loyalty to the Harrow Company that kept them going.

Once the immediate crisis passed, the day-to-day involvement of these managers was essential to keep the business moving forward. Their rationalizations about Newcomb's style were beginning to wear thin; it was getting harder to be convinced that her self-centered attitude had redeeming value. Morale was bad and the team lacked its usual winning spirit.

The recruiting world has a knack for knowing where talent is ripe for the picking; job offers found their way into the organization and the exodus began. This negative fallout filtered down to the rank and file in the plant and a historically constructive relationship with the union began to go sour.

Top management found the loss of talent even more disturbing than the sluggish business results. Profits can be recovered, but it takes years to build a capable and dedicated work force. The CEO was deeply concerned. Newcomb was a capable manager who had done wonders with the business. However, she was having her troubles — and there were no clear solutions. Newcomb was not a mean person. In fact, her behavior would not be a problem in most other organizations. At Harrow, her management style was drastically different from what the people had learned to expect from their leaders. The CEO, a staunch proponent of the established management credo, concluded that the root of the problem was how Newcomb was treating her people. Because Newcomb was cut from such a different cloth, she was asked to leave.

We've Got to Change the Way We Treat People

A clash with corporate culture also arises when a new manager is out to change "the way we treat people around here." At Craig Securities, Bob Lamm found himself faced with such a situation. His new boss wanted the back office reorganized to get costs on a par with the competition. This strategy dictated a personnel philosophy that would allow people to lose their jobs. Historically employees never had to fear for their jobs. Lamm saw himself as a protector of the people.

The new boss had a different outlook on the company's obligations to employees. She was being paid to increase profits, not to nurture a familial organization. She was not indifferent to the disruption she would be stirring in the lives of these people, but her responsibility was to restore the firm's economic viability. Job elimination was an essential and legitimate course of action.

In the end, Lamm was fired for refusing to implement the boss's strategy of automating the back office operation. His resistance was based on his commitment to protect the jobs of loyal employees. The strategies and philosophical questions are so intertwined that one would have to say that they were both fundamental to the clash between Lamm and his new boss.

BLATANT ANTAGONISM IS TROUBLE IN MOST CULTURES

Some individuals have a knack for making other people angry. Wherever they go, sooner or later, the antagonist manages to raise the ire of a wide range of personalities. They go against the grain of the prevailing management ideal of most organizations — a cooperative spirit. Most managers have limited tolerance for disruptive types. The larger the organization, the lower the tolerance for antagonism.

There are several types of antagonists. The most blatant are those filled with anger and hostility, quick to lash out at others. Less vicious in nature is the person who always seems to say the wrong thing — inadvertently hurting feelings or bruising egos. Self-centered individuals with large egos leave little room for the ideas or needs of others. Then there are those people who feel compelled to impose their will on others. Let's look at this sampling of antagonists in action.

Rebel in Search of a Cause

Ted Moran was exquisite during the employment interviews. His answers were intelligent and wise, reflecting the current wisdom of effective management and the state of the art in strategic planning. On top of this, he exuded just the right air of confidence and executive demeanor. A bit more assertive and opinionated than typically found in the organization, but change is what management wanted. Moran was hired to nudge the organization forward.

The company was successful in growing its own talent. As a normal side effect of inbreeding, the diversity of personalities and values in the organization had narrowed. There was a cohesive effort to maintain the status quo. Thus management was attracted to someone with the gumption to push for change.

The mandate for change was openly discussed and presumably understood from the beginning. Management's unspoken mandate was: "Help us gradually make a transition." Moran took their mandate as a license to kill.

Moran was going to show them the way. Instead of waiting to get to know the organization and giving the people a chance to know him, he told them in no uncertain terms that their approach to planning was wrong. He made no attempt to find out why things were done the way they were or why change had been resisted for so long. He never stopped to recognize that the organization's approach to planning was a reflection of how they viewed the world.

He staked out his position and held hard. Things had to be his way or no way at all. He was so rigid that there was no room for compromise. The organization had no choice but to fight back.

However, the organization did not respond in kind to his strongly worded, authoritative statements. They were unaccustomed to fighting against an aggressive foe. The stranger from the outside quickly became an enemy who galvanized the organization to pull together against him.

Even the members of senior management who recognized the validity of Moran's ideas began to feel that the constant skirmishes were intolerable. Besides, it was becoming evident that the desired change was not going to come about through this rambunctious agent. Their plan was abandoned and Moran had to find a new battleground.

The Expert Always Knows Best

Among the high-tech firms on the outer ring of Boston is Kezing Corporation, a specialist in industrial optics. Having ventured into laser beam technology, they found themselves in need of a sophisticated technician to develop products. A difficult and frustrating search dragged on for 10 months, until they discovered Marion Sharp.

Sharp, a technical wizard, was uniquely qualified to thrust them into this explosive market. Her manager, vice president of research and development, was pleased. It was evident early in the interview process that Sharp did not always get along well with others. This didn't disturb her boss, who was used to working with prima donnas. He valued their technical contributions and learned to live with their foibles.

Sharp's extraordinary level of expertise in this new technology made her unique and special. This went to her head and gave her an inflated sense of importance. She made no attempt to feign modesty and wore her superiority with a brassiness that was annoying. She didn't hesitate to tell people what she thought of their ideas. If she thought they were wrong, she told them so in no uncertain terms. She just didn't concern herself with how people might feel about her — or how she made them feel about themselves.

Sharp was not an angry person out to antagonize the world. She just did not go through the trouble to make her criticism palatable to recipients. In her mind, the ultimate authority was scientific truth; organizational relationships had no bearing on the solution to problems. Sensitivity to others was just not part of her makeup. On a number of occasions, her manager had to smooth over the inevitable friction. Sharp's manager traded off the disruptions against the expertise gained by the organization.

After three years, however, there was a major reorganization. Sharp found herself reporting to a different boss — a member of top management. The new boss didn't have the time or patience to help high-priced people get along with each other. She also found Sharp's arrogance to be insufferable. Within six months of reporting to her new boss, Sharp was fired.

The Marines Have Landed

Kurt Krieger was a top-flight manufacturing executive — a tough, demanding, no-nonsense manager. ND Industries hired him to modernize their fastest growing facility. His experience with other manufacturing companies gave him the knowledge needed to do the job.

Krieger wasn't always the easiest guy to get along with. He loved a good fight. His urge to do battle often overpowered his political instincts. Interpersonal style aside, Krieger was a sharp, astute individual with uncanny intuition when it came to manufacturing problems. He was rarely proven wrong.

During his first six months on the job, he gained the respect of the management team. They came to expect his readiness to take on a fight, but accepted this as part of the package. It was a small price to pay for the much-needed improvements. Krieger exceeded his boss's hopes and expectations — production capacity and efficiency were at all-time highs.

Eventually, Krieger began to help other divisions solve their manufacturing problems. His boss, rather than being threatened, took pride in this. Besides, Krieger never forgot who was the boss. Unfortunately, Krieger's propensity to take on sparring partners was not so well received by his technical counterparts in the other divisions.

The manufacturing executives at the corporate office were distressed by the friction Krieger caused. They had worked hard to build cohesion and a cooperative spirit among the various engineers in the company. From their perspective, his incessant disruptiveness outweighed his value to the organization. His boss was compelled to yield to the higher powers in the company. In spite of his technical capability, Krieger was asked to leave.

As noted earlier, most organizations have little tolerance for someone with a sharply antagonistic nature. Such individuals are usually screened out somewhere along the way. The antagonist is his own worst enemy: survival depends on having a boss who is not threatened or put off by an antagonistic style. Many antagonists are aware of their propensity to make people angry; some have learned to curb their behavior with the boss.

WHEN ARE PHILOSOPHICAL DIFFERENCES FATAL?

Each of the cases discussed involved an executive who was at odds with a boss's management philosophy. Does this mean someone's job is automatically at risk if they don't embrace the boss's management ideals? Is there no room for divergence in this world of ever-changing values? Not necessarily. In these cases of employees being terminated because of a philosophical clash with a new boss, certain critical conditions were always present. Either the boss considered his or her own philosophy to be essential to success or the subordinate's approach to people resulted in organizational disruption.

In certain instances the boss believed that the subordinate's philosophy was a major stumbling block to executing the business strategy. Roland, the new CEO at Home Products, was convinced that Marks's tight control was preventing the business from being competitive. Roland also believed that if managers were unaware of the importance of market share, the business would never gain the competitive superiority needed for healthy long-term profits. All in all, he considered the shift to his management ideals essential to business success.

The same was true at Craig Securities. Lamm's loyalty to the work force stood in the way of streamlining the operation. Lamm's new boss was not against building the good will and trust of employees. However, she believed that in the long run no one's job would be protected if operating costs were not brought down to competitive levels. Lamm became an obstacle to doing what the boss considered to be fundamental to future business profits.

The other condition under which a philosophical dispute proved terminal was when the subordinate's deviation caused significant disruption within the organization. At Argus Industries, senior management felt compelled to terminate Henderson only after divisional management started fighting over the personnel department's tight administrative control. Too much time and energy was being consumed by battles over this conflict. While it was not truly fundamental to the success of the business, peace among the money earners certainly had its virtues.

Noland's fate at Kane Corporation closely paralleled the Argus case. A certain amount of conflict between division management and corporate staff is inevitable and is usually accepted as a normal state of affairs. Noland went beyond the bounds of normal friction, and the disruption caused within the organization became intolerable to the boss.

At Harrow, the CEO believed that Newcomb's autocratic, self-centered style was undermining morale and costing the company valuable talent. Without the wholehearted support of the organization Newcomb could not break through the stubborn sales plateau. The organizational disruption was seen as the culprit in preventing good business results. Both of the critical conditions were present: unacceptable organizational strife and an obstacle to good results.

Chapter Six

Who Expects What
From Whom

Conflict Over Organizational Roles

A senior executive was hired to head up the mergers and acquisition effort of a multibillion-dollar corporation. With his usual aggressiveness and determination, he analyzed prospective acquisitions and proceeded to cut deals. Unfortunately for him, there was one little fact that he did not understand: He was only supposed to screen and politely reject the various and sundry unsolicited proposals that came across the transom — the adventure of pursuing acquisitions was a privilege reserved for the CEO and nobody else. The acquisition expert was fired for performing the wrong role.

A subordinate is expected to fulfill a certain role in the organization. This role is usually based on a specific notion of how the subordinate should complement the boss's efforts. When their respective roles do not fit together, termination is often a solution to the conflict.

The cases in this chapter are typical of the ways a subordinate can fall dangerously outside a boss's role expectations. Personality is an ever-present influence on the attitudes people have about their own role and what they expect from others. As will be evident from the following cases, human chemistry aside, certain jobs in a corporation carry a higher than average risk for the occupant.

THE PRECARIOUS ROLE OF THE GROUP EXECUTIVE

At top corporate levels, one of the most problematic roles is that of the group executive. The group executive typically reports to the president and is responsible for a group of businesses. Simply put, both the president and the general manager of each business are ultimately accountable for the results of the business. And so is the group executive!

Where does the group executive fit? Does he serve as strategic guru, standing on the sidelines with a scorecard and watching the division heads manage their businesses? Does he step in and tell them how to run their operations? Is he simply a high-priced communication link between the president and the general managers? Where is the line drawn? How many different executives can be in charge of the same business? What are the odds of all three levels being in synch about strategy and management philosophy?

Carl Jenkins was hired by Diversified Industries to be the group executive over two of their business sectors, small household appliances and industrial machine tools. The appliance area was old hat for him: He was recruited from the biggest competitor in the industry. He had a firm grasp of each competitor's movements, understood the technology, and was tuned in to the consumer. On the other hand, he had no experience with industrial tools, so this business offered him the excitement of mastering a new field.

In the screening process, top management was impressed with Jenkins's experience. He had done well in managing sizable profit centers within other large corporate environments and intimately knew the appliance industry. Certain admirable qualities were readily apparent, including a keen business sense, a broad perspective, and self-confidence. He appeared to be a talented executive who was a comfortable fit.

Given his accomplishments and reputation, the chief executive, Warren Baxter, considered him a top contender for the corporate presidency. This view suited Jenkins just fine—his sights were set on the top job. Interestingly, in spite of their subsequent falling out, Baxter, still does not doubt that Jenkins has the capacity to run a major corporation.

As a broad-gauged executive, Jenkins sought to oversee the general direction of the business. This was easy for him to do in the appliance business without ever getting into the day-to-day details of the business. Jenkins followed the same approach with the unfamiliar machine tool business. He gained an overview of where the business was going and how it was trying to get there, but he relied on the division president to worry about the details of the business.

After the initial honeymoon, Baxter started to query Jenkins about the two businesses. They had a grand time talking about the appliance business, but things weren't so smooth when the subject shifted to the machine tool business. Baxter could never figure out how much Jenkins knew about what was going on in that business.

He began to get the feeling that Jenkins was trying to bluff his way through. The harder he pressed for answers, the more the tension built.

Baxter wanted the group executives to master all the ins and outs of the various businesses and to provide ongoing guidance to the general managers. With the group executives giving close attention to the running of the businesses, Baxter could step back and focus on the broad strategic issues. Jenkins also sought to act like a distant overseer. Thus, contrary to Baxter's desire, Jenkins did not get close to the action. He felt that he was involved enough in the businesses to be effective. To compound the problem, being so unfamiliar with the machine tool industry, he avoided spending time with that business.

The human resources executive attempted to bridge the growing gap between Baxter and Jenkins. He tried to get Jenkins to consider the possibility that his knowledge of the industrial sector might be too superficial. Jenkins was adamant that he knew what he was doing in his job. He became defensive and closed to the counsel of others. As the final recourse to undo this unacceptable situation, Jenkins was terminated.

In retrospect, management feels that Jenkins's unfamiliarity with the tool business should have been faced as soon as he came on board. Management should have reached an understanding about how Jenkins would overcome this knowledge gap and make the transition into serving an active role in managing the business. If such preventive measures had been taken before relationships became severely strained, Jenkins might still be there today — as president and chief operating officer.

Frank Parker's situation at Chemtech Corporation paralleled Jenkins's plight. While Parker and his boss could not see eye to eye on strategy, their conflict also was related to their opposing views of how much time the group executive should spend in the field. Had Parker dug into the details of his businesses, their differences over strategy might not have been so far apart. They battled over strategy — their conflicting role expectations should have been resolved first.

The clash at Clarity Limited between Joanne Locke, the group executive, and Charles Kheel, the division president, also involved role conflict. The crux of their battle was incompatible beliefs about how far to take the business. At another level, though, the conflict concerned a group executive's struggle to exert the authority of her role. Each was giving direction to the organization — but who was in charge? As Locke put more pressure on getting her ideas into motion, the organization began to act like a tormented two-headed monster. The conflict of wills over strategy became a clash over role dominance.

These cases show how precarious life can be for a group executive. However, a word of caution is in order for division presidents about to play the "let's undermine the new group executive's authority" game. Many years of a seemingly strong relationship with top management may cause managers to take their job security for granted. Acting on presumed loyalty, a manager may discover too late that the group executive was brought in with a mandate and a free hand to fix the ills of the business. The unsuspecting manager might have been fingered as part of the problem. A new group executive's suggestions may sound like friendly advice instead of an order, but a blatant disregard for his words of wisdom may prove fatal.

MOVING INTO THE TOP
JOB—ALMOST

The landscape is littered with evidence that chief executives are often faced with the group executive's conflicting expectations about what role they should serve. Presidents often assume that they were hired to run the company and perhaps even to succeed a chairman nearing retirement. After months of frustration and anguish, it becomes apparent that the CEO is not prepared to relinquish the role.

There is particular risk for the strong leader hired to manage a business under a long-tenured CEO. After years of seeing a business through thick and thin, a CEO can become possessive. Even when an executive knows in his own mind that another leader needs to be put in charge, it may be difficult for the body and soul to let go. A persistent struggle for custody of a business is resolved by an involuntary expulsion from the leader's territory.

THE NEW BREED OF STRATEGIC PLANNER

In the 1970s, strategic planning emerged as an influential function within corporations. Organizations hired sophisticated planning professionals to develop long-term strategic plans. Planning departments grew in stature, influence, and size. A natural conflict developed between the staff planner and the line manager: Who is responsible for developing strategy? The burgeoning role of the professional planner began to decline and corporate planning departments were slashed in size. The survivors were the professionals who could help line managers without attempting to be the architect of the plan. Many capable planners who were unable to make this transition were victims of a drastic change in role expectations.

Jeff Noland at Kane Corporation is a prime example. Noland was considered an excellent strategist and planner. There was unanimous consensus that the planning process he put into place was invaluable—the techniques are still in use years after his departure. No one ever took issue with his technical competence. He got into trouble when he attempted to use his role in the planning process to establish a power base. It was evident that the role of planning czar was dysfunctional and Noland was never replaced.

The strategic planning evolution has put the jobs of

capable executives at risk. Individuals who have performed effectively for years may wake up one morning to discover that a changing world has rendered them superfluous. It is often a new boss who announces the dawning of the transition.

WHAT DOES YOUR HUMAN RESOURCE EXECUTIVE DO FOR YOU?

Few roles have changed as drastically as personnel's. Over the years, the financial consequences and complications of civil rights, pension laws, and other legislation did much to transform the function. Even going beyond these issues, modern management has come to recognize the importance of human resources in the overall management of the business. This has created a demand for business-oriented professionals who can contribute to the running of the business.

The problem for the human resource professional is that companies have not uniformly made this transition; there is enormous variability in what different managers expect from the human resource function. This diversity places the human resource professional in a precarious position — especially when confronted with a new boss. A subordinate never knows what role the next boss will want him to serve. Even without a change in boss, the professional may find that the leader has drastically changed his expectations.

Snacks Unlimited had grown into a phenomenal fast-food chain with units all over the world.

Rapid growth, when you are 10 steps ahead of the competition, can be a gold mine. Management imperfections are easily ignored and absorbed by the gush of cash flow. While the rigors of careful budgeting and planning can be essential to a mature business struggling to hold onto narrow profit margins, these disciplines do not seem so critical when the business is enjoying easy riches.

At Snacks Unlimited, the same attitude extended to the management of human resources. There was plenty of excess wealth to cover any sins, such as not planning future management needs. So much of their success rested on the genius of their founding leader that little attention was paid to building the management ranks.

Julia Hill had managed the human resource department for six years, doing no more and no less than what top management wanted from her. Then one cloudy morning her leader woke up from a sleepless night; he had been tossing and turning, worrying about what would happen if the magic bubble burst. He became concerned about the company's ability to be managed through any difficult times that may lie ahead, and what would happen when he eventually retired. Would succeeding management do justice to the legacy and enable the legend — and the high stock price — to live on?

This cast a new light on the human resource function: Management succession, manpower planning, training and development were no longer irrelevant. The human resource function became vital to the company. Since Hill was not skilled in these areas, she was replaced. The new human resource officer was a contemporary professional—seasoned in the new wave of thinking—who could accomplish the leader's goals. Hill was a competent performer—until her role changed.

A new personnel executive at Star Broadcasting Company was charged with the task of achieving a similar reorientation. His head of training and development, George Brewer, was a conscientious administrator who efficiently ran training sessions, maintained career summaries on employees, and kept records meticulously up-to-date. He was well received by both corporate and division management, owing in part to his responsiveness and pleasant manner. An avid reader, Brewer was current on recent developments in the field. Unfortunately, in spite of his knowledge and good relationships, he was unable to establish himself as an advisor to management. He knew what was written in the management development field, but did not have the consultative skills for translating the principles into action. Since manpower development was an ideal avenue for transforming the role of personnel at the broadcasting company, Brewer was replaced.

When Barbara Evans came to work for the regional manager of Casualty Insurance Company, she was not faced with the risk of a new manager. She had worked for this manager before and they had a common understanding of what would be expected from her. After a secure couple of years, her manager and mentor moved on.

The woman who took her manager's place was pleased with Evans's extensive personnel experience. They worked well together. Eventually, the new regional manager found that many of the local offices were not well managed. Supervisors didn't know how to stay on top of problems, turnover was hurting relationships with independent brokers, and the quality of personnel decisions was inconsistent. This made it imperative that the human resource professional be able to counsel line managers on how to hire, train, and manage their people. Even the regional manager wanted to have someone serve as a sounding board.

Evans was better than most at installing and administering formal personnel programs, but she was not skilled in counseling managers to think through their decisions about people. Evans was a perfect fit for what many corporations look for from their personnel departments, but not a good match for this new manager. After trying to make a go of it for a number of months, Evans finally found herself faced with the task of finding one of those better matches.

Did the termination of Hill, Brewer, and Evans mean that they were not competent professionals? They all enjoyed good progress in the personnel field. They were hard working, dedicated, and productive individuals who could be relied on to get things done according to plan. However, none of them were seasoned counselors and they could not serve as advisor and confidant to top management. When greater sophistication became a fundamental requisite of the role, these praiseworthy professionals had to seek their fortunes elsewhere.

At Hometown Savings Bank, Bill Cantor was to discover that the pendulum can swing in the other direction. Over the past few years, Cantor had been instrumental in helping his president execute a difficult turnaround of a failing bank. It involved drastic personnel cuts, many executive replacements, and innovative changes in the corporate structure. Cantor was the president's right-hand man in planning these organizational changes, working closely with all levels of management to implement the plan. Ironically, having a strategic business orientation, he just might have been the perfect replacement for any one of the other three terminated professionals.

Then the bank was acquired by an overseas holding company that took an active hand in the turnaround and Cantor found himself with a new boss. The new president was an exceedingly self-reliant individual. He had great faith in his own ability to make astute personnel judgments and felt little need for advice on such matters. This left Cantor with a mere skeleton of his former job. To make matters worse, his attempts to offer advice were not well received. When he tactfully challenged any conclusions — a role always welcomed by the prior president — their relationship took a decided turn for the worse. Whether he could have been valuable to the new president became moot. Cantor found himself looking for a new job — and a boss who wanted what he had to offer.

LEAD TO YOUR BOSS'S WEAKNESS

When the top financial officer of Consolidated National was elected president, he hired Richard Strawbridge to fill the position he was vacating. Wanting someone who could function effectively at the senior level of this complex corporation, he recruited Strawbridge away from another multinational giant. Strawbridge's strength was first and foremost in the controllership area, having exceptional experience in installing and managing complex financial systems for manufacturing businesses. In spite of his extensive financial experience, Strawbridge had never been directly involved in raising capital or investing funds.

Putting his expertise immediately to work, Strawbridge installed a new companywide accounting system for close monitoring of their diverse operations. He also revitalized the audit function. He kept a sharp eye on costs and operating problems.

Strawbridge and the president had a superb working relationship; each was a natural complement of the other. While Strawbridge covered the administration of corporate accounting, the president handled strategic financial issues. Given his own limited experience in the treasury side, Strawbridge was just as happy to let his boss worry about the company's intricate financial arrangements and complex capital structure. Strawbridge was the inside man; the president focused on external financial questions. Each executive led to his own strengths and stayed away from the activities each preferred to avoid. It was a perfect complementary relationship—a natural foundation for a strong partnership.

Four years later the president left for greener pastures and the head of the corporation's largest subsidiary took his place. The replacement had good financial acumen, but saw his role as being that of general management. He sought to devote all his time to overseeing the operating businesses and charting their future growth. This left a critical void in the company: Who would handle the financing of the growth?

Strawbridge was comfortable enough keeping on top of the machinery for monitoring the operations, but he had neither the experience nor the inclination to mastermind complex financial deals. The new president, in order to lead to his particular strengths, needed an executive who could cover all aspects of the financial function.

The change in presidents created a mismatch — the boss and the subordinate were functionally incompatible. After four years of strong performance, this otherwise capable financial executive, who had made significant contributions to the company, could not meet the new boss's role expectations and had to find a compatible match elsewhere.

The ideal situation is to be highly skilled in those areas in which the boss admits to being weak. Conversely, having the same functional strengths as a boss has the potential for breeding a competitive relationship. If the boss feels threatened and insists on being the organization's top expert in your particular area of specialization, your situation can be both frustrating and tenuous.

PERSPECTIVE FOR THE LINE EXECUTIVE

Terminated line executives are not necessarily deficient in their leadership skills; it is more often a question of how they go about taking on the role of leader. Some get into trouble when they attempt to exert too much leadership and infringe on the boss's territory. Others fail to become involved enough in the details of their operations: The boss wants someone to take a more active role in the day-to-day management of the business. It's not that any of these executives are not effective leaders, but rather that their assumptions about their leadership role conflicted with the boss's expectations.

The person who especially needs to be alert to this problem is the line executive in charge of a business — the chief operating officer, the group executive, or the division president. Each has a boss who is fully accountable for the subordinate's business.

When moving into one of these general management positions, the definition of the job may seem obvious to both the boss and the subordinate — to be in charge of the business. The compatibility of their expectations is usually taken for granted; rarely do the parties attempt to verify whether they are both talking about the same role. Yet, as is evident from the case histories, clearly defining management roles is not always simple and conflicting expectations can end in termination.

Some of the cases involved a conflict over power and authority. The line between what's mine and what's yours is not always drawn. There may not be any "do not trespass" signs warning where not to tread, but the sacred bounds of the boss's territory may nonetheless be wired with lethal voltage. Many a boss takes a "watch and see" attitude, waiting for the subordinate to read his mind. When the boss knows he shouldn't be holding the reins so tightly, he may not want to come right out and tell the subordinate to fall in line. Then again, the boss who freely talks about wanting an executive who can take over may be sending a false signal. Either way, there is no warning that the mine field is filled with charges waiting to explode.

In summary, when taking on new line management responsibilities, it is important to clarify assumptions and expectations about the role to be served before signing on the dotted line. This means verifying how much authority goes with the position and what kind of leadership role is considered critical to effectively manage the operations. Whenever the boss's behavior seems out of kilter with that understanding, the incongruities should be dealt with out in the open. It is important to gauge if time is likely to soften the boss's tight hold on the reins. When it is necessary to push hard to gain control, it may also be prudent to begin laying the groundwork for pursuing alternative career options rather than waiting to be forced to do so on the boss's terms.

WHEN THE STAFF ROLE IS OUT OF SYNCH

For the staff person, a change in boss offers the possibility of a misfit and a potential threat to job security — regardless of tenure, experience, and potential. Henceforth life will be different, for better or worse.

When the staff person is considering going to work for a different boss, both parties have the opportunity to evaluate the match beforehand. However, when the boss is the one taking the new job, only time will tell if the staff person can meet the new boss's expectations. How can staff tell if trouble is afoot so that they can plan their lives accordingly?

Instructive patterns do emerge from the case studies. In broad terms, certain managers look for staff professionals to participate in thinking through strategic questions. They expect their staff to play an active role in various aspects of planning and strategic problem solving. Sharp lines are not drawn between staff and line managers — they are expected to participate as a team.

Other managers feel that their job, as the singular leader, is to develop the strategy for the business and to personally solve any problems of consequence. The role of staff is to execute the vision — not help shape it. This requires doers and administrators who can execute programs and efficiently manage departments. "I'll do the thinking; you get it done."

In reviewing the cases of staff mismatches, the boss invariably had a strong preference for either the strategist or the administrator. Strawbridge was hired for his administrative skills and fired by a boss who wanted a broader financial executive. Hill, Brewer, and Evans were all knowledgeable human resource professionals who efficiently kept personnel programs and transactions on track; in these cases replacements were sought who could influence how the organization should be managed.

A change in boss can shift the emphasis of a staff role overnight. A hero to one manager may end up being a loser to the next. If the strengths don't line up with the boss's orientation, then it's time to map out career alternatives. Forcing a fit that is not meant to be can do awful things to the nerves and blood pressure. Objectively recognizing a mismatch is better for one's self-esteem than waiting for a boss to chip away at the imperfections in the fit. Besides, why wait till the boss decides that your paychecks are about to stop coming home?

Chapter Seven

I Have Seen the Enemy

How to Take Command of Your Future

A re you caught in a difficult clash with your boss? Is termination inevitable? Can you reconcile your differences? Is your job worth saving? Should you try? What should you do about it?

This chapter deals with the actions that an individual can take to stay in command of his or her career. There are no magic prescriptions. The guiding principle is to help the individual to be objective and realistic in assessing the risks and the opportunities. The ultimate goal is to be the one who chooses from the alternatives rather than leaving the choice completely up to someone else.

First, a series of recommended actions are provided for analyzing a current job situation and dealing with an ongoing relationship with a boss. Second, a set of suggestions is provided for the person about to enter into a relationship with a new boss. In both instances, the perspective is from the point of view of the individual; the final chapter deals with what the boss — management — can do to prevent wasteful firings.

THE RELATIONSHIP WITH THE BOSS — REALISM AND CONSTRUCTIVE ACTION

Don't Assume It Can't Happen to You

Research and experience say that it can happen to anyone — the brightest stars, the high potential executives, the top performers — even after years of dedication to a company. No one is guaranteed immunity. Many leaders, with careers and successes most people would love to emulate, have been fired along the way.

Stepping back from the individual situation, firings can appear to be random hits. One person fired just after starting a new job and another after 15 years of service; some young, others old; the dedicated as well as the disloyal; the smooth along with the abrasive. So why should you believe that you are somehow immune?

You may believe that it doesn't happen in your company. In some organizations it can be difficult, if not almost impossible to get fired. Yet even these rare companies find a way to move undesired employees out of the way. Much like the human body, an organization naturally defends itself against antagonistic or threatening forces — they are isolated and neutralized until dispelled. Even if a company has staunchly maintained a protective attitude for decades, the most embedded rules can change overnight — especially when performance declines and a new leader is dropped into place to fix things. Futhermore, these days no company is safe from being swallowed up by another; then it's a case of new bosses on a grand scale.

This warning does not mean that you should become suspicious of a boss's every move. Accept the reality that you can be at risk and don't be blinded by overconfidence, pride, or egotism. There's nothing wrong with staying in touch with changes in your environment that can trigger a need to readapt. Don't make any false assumptions about your situation — you want to stay in command of your future!

Determine Your Risk Quotient

Certain kinds of situations can significantly heighten a person's risk of termination. Failure to get the job done is obviously one way to tempt the fates, but beyond this it is important to recognize the kinds of changes that can shift your risk past the red line into the danger zone.

Throughout this book, it has been stressed that the one thing most terminated individuals have in common is having been fired by someone who has only just recently become their boss. When you take a new job, you invariably have a new boss—so the same principle applies. The wider the differences in your experiences and perspectives, the greater the risk for misunderstandings and possible breakdowns. If you worked previously with the new boss, there is less likely to be any surprises.

If you have moved to a different company and therefore have entered a new culture, your adaptation is a hurdle that can make or break your success. If your new boss has been part of the culture for a long period of time and has become an assimilated member, then the mastery of the prevailing culture is critical. Your entry as a foreign, unknown element introduces a certain degree of instability. Until accommodation and assimilation are achieved, you are at risk.

When a new leader is put in charge of an organization, there is instant instability. Events in an organization become unpredictable when there is instability—things are shaken up and people are shaken out until stability is reestablished. If a new boss is put in directly over you, it is time to be alert and vigilant. If there is a new leader a level or two above your boss, the waves of change will flow down the steps of the organization chart. It may happen gradually or fall like a thundering waterfall.

Beyond the new boss–new job situation, watch for

drastic events that can destabilize an organization — a sharp downturn in results, overpowering competitive threats, or a foreboding economic climate. A shakeup in an industry will find its way into the internal workings of an organization.

Instability changes the rules; events are less predictable. Acting on old assumptions is more frivolous than ever before. Instability, especially with a new leader, can trigger new ways of looking at where the business is going and how it should get there. This opens the door for conflict. Your ideas about business strategy, management philosophy, and your role may become out of synch with the changes taking place around you.

You should test your risk quotient periodically. Are you in one of those high risk situations in which anyone, regardless of ability, could be in danger? Keep in mind that high risk events — new job, new boss, or instability of the company — are also times of opportunity. Proceed with your eyes wide open and be alert for indications that the ice is getting thin.

Look for the Danger Signs

If you are in a high risk situation, the next step is to find out if you are in danger. There is no sure way of knowing whether you are marked for termination, but there are danger signs to indicate if you are on your way to becoming an outsider.

When your boss is comfortable with who you are, what you are doing, and how you are doing it, there is a sense of well-being. This doesn't mean that there is a lack of challenge or stress, but at least the fit feels right.

At the other extreme is the boss who is dissatisfied with the fit and predisposed to your termination. No matter what you do, you can't seem to get on the right side of the boss. When an organization is moving closer to your removal, people send inconsistent signals. Things just aren't fitting together the way they should. You experience unusual discomfort or apprehension. The tension may be hard to define—a vague sense that all is not right in the world. You may not even feel up to par physically—lacking energy, tiring easily, or even susceptible to getting sick. You may be worn out from fighting an invisible enemy.

If you are not sure whether your situation is tenuous, listen carefully to your instincts. Stress can be caused by any number of things, but if your manager is thinking of firing you and you don't know it, this certainly could be a cause of ill-defined anxiety. Some questions you should ask yourself are:

Is your boss spending less time with you?

Is the interaction less relaxed? More formal? Strained?

Are you not being brought in on things as much as you used to or should expect to be?

Has the boss started to turn to other people to get things done that were usually in your purview?

Has the boss started to build the organization around you—in effect acting as though you were already gone?

Is the boss or are others in the organization directly

accessing your subordinates? Is this a departure from past practice?

Is there a freeze on your decisions, with requests frequently denied and prerogatives challenged?

Are you precluded from making major changes — be it reorganization, hiring, or starting new projects? Do you seem to be in a holding pattern, pending you don't know what?

Have people in the organization become increasingly resistant to your ideas and actions?

Do you sense that your influence on your own staff has seriously diminished — much like a lame duck?

Listen carefully to what is being said and what is not being said. Don't ignore your instincts. Your sixth sense may help fill in the gaps that your eyes and ears do not pick up directly — the writing that is not on the wall. Some do this better than others, depending on how in touch they are with their feelings. The signals of danger can be sensed without knowing the shape of the enemy.

Spouses can have an uncanny ability to pick up the subtle changes in a mate undergoing the stress of a threatening job situation. They may be able to translate the meaning of these warning signals more readily than the one caught in the middle of it all. If your spouse starts to tell you that it doesn't sound like things are going so well for you at the office, don't be so quick to come with a short-tempered, "What do you mean, if there was something wrong at work wouldn't I know about it!" If your spouse is forever insecure about your progress, that is another matter. Otherwise, take heed if your spouse senses that something is wrong — especially when you find yourself being irritated by the concerns.

Don't become overly suspicious, looking for demons behind every desk. However, if you're in an unstable situation, give due consideration to the danger signals. You want to be able to deal effectively with the realities of the situation and move to your advantage.

Pinpoint the Underlying Conflict

Having decided that your relationship with the boss has gone sour is one thing; figuring out why you are at odds is another. If you are going to be able to determine if reconciliation is desirable or feasible, you need to understand the specific points of difference that have caused your boss to decide that you are not wanted on the team. Using the framework provided in the previous chapters, go through each type of potential conflict to identify the possible areas of incompatibility with your boss.

Personality. Are you caught in a personality clash with your boss? The various danger signs discussed earlier are all clues to a problematic fit with a manager. Unless the boss comes right out and tells you, it is difficult to assess the reason for the bad chemistry. You may never know whether initial differences over business issues eventually erupted into a disintegration of the relationship or whether an ill-fated relationship created a heightened sensitivity to any differences. The best you can do is recognize that the relationship is one of the areas that may be placing your job in jeopardy.

Business Strategy. Are there significant differences

in where you think the business should go and how it should get there? Are there issues concerning such things as the size of the potential market, speed of growth, staffing levels, use of technology, cost control, or risk taking? Incompatible differences over the strategic direction of the organization can result in a volatile situation. You need to assess the chances of your boss being won over to your viewpoint — your future in this job may depend on it.

Management Philosophy. Are you clashing over philosophical differences? No two people are likely to be identical in their beliefs about how an organization should be managed and particularly how people should be treated. Problems arise when you act against a boss's deeply held ideals. The danger is greatest when the boss believes that your approach will not produce the desired business results or when your behavior is disruptive to the organization. You need to identify the fundamental underlying constructs which the boss considers essential to the effective functioning of the organization and determine if you are fighting against what the boss considers to be self-evident truths.

Does your boss take exception to how you handle people?

Is your approach to managing the organization diametrically opposed to the boss's?

Are you departing from patterns long established in the organization?

Are people resisting your attempts to change the way the organization functions?

Do you frequently get into disagreements with people in the organization?

Do you sense that the organization, as well as the boss, finds you to be an antagonistic force?

Organizational Role. Do you and your boss have different ideas about the role you should be fulfilling?

Are you frustrated over the boundaries the boss imposes on your role?

Do you infringe on each other's efforts to lead the organization?

Are your strengths well suited to the boss's concept of your role?

What reason do you have to believe that you and your boss have a common view of the role you should be fulfilling?

Try to sort through the incompatibilities that may be getting in your way. Unless the differences are readily apparent, you might try writing out a list of your views in one column and your boss's in another. This list could cover your respective ideas on business strategy, management philosophy, and organizational roles. Then you could search through for the critical differences that might be getting in the way of a compatible working relationship.

Know Thyself

To fully understand why you may be on a collision course, it is important to take a clear and objective look at both you and your boss. Starting with a self-assessment, you need a handle on:

Your strengths and limitations

Your style of working, thinking, decision making, and leading

Your approach to managing an organization and relating with people

Your beliefs about the company's business strategy, the organization, and your role

Then consider how well you fit the current situation:

Are you well suited to perform your job?

Have you kept pace with any changes in the demands of your job?

Is your style of working, thinking, deciding, and leading effective in this organization?

Are your beliefs, values, and ideas in synch with those around you?

Are you able to thrive and be at your best in the current situation?

Self-assessment is easier said than done, especially if you are caught in a conflict with your boss. There are forces at play that may be working against your having an objective picture of yourself. If your boss has a negative attitude toward you, this will invariably have some effect on how you see yourself. Your manager's negative expectations can cause you to have self-doubts or, at the opposite extreme, you may adopt a protective posture of overconfidence. Either reaction robs you of the ability to objectively and realistically deal with your situation.

A third-party viewpoint can be helpful. It is important to be able to turn to someone who is willing to be honest and if necessary critical. Sometimes well-meaning people hold back out of a misguided concern for your feelings. Futhermore, it is especially difficult to know if someone within your organization is being objective or completely honest with you. A good friend or associate outside the environment often can provide the best counsel.

Know Thy Boss

The corollary to knowing thyself is knowing where your boss is coming from. To understand why you are colliding with your manager, you need a grasp of how this human being sees the world. The process of stepping back from this person, attempting to figure him out so to speak, can help your mind get a healthier distance away from the relationship, and thereby better equip you to sort out the world that is impinging with seeming impunity on your life.

The assessment should follow the same questions asked in assessing yourself:

What are your boss's strengths and weaknesses?

What is your boss's style of working, thinking, decision making, and leading?

Does your boss represent an extreme of any particular style? Is this person likely to tolerate a diametrically opposite approach?

What are your manager's beliefs about business strategy, management philosophy, and your respective roles.

When you complete your assessment of the boss, look for your similarities and differences. Are there basic differences in style or temperament that help explain any disagreements or conflicts that may have erupted? The ultimate objective is to understand what is happening to you, why, and what you should do about it.

Before attempting to fix it you should ask two more questions:

Is your job salvageable?

Is it really to your advantage to save it?

Both of these questions may be easier to answer after you have attempted to straighten things out. Nonetheless, this is the point at which you should recognize that these are legitimate questions — especially if you hold the view that you are the commander of your life and not simply a victim.

Are You Past the Point of No Return?

When the boss, along with other key players in the organization, becomes convinced that you do not fit in, the dynamics and momentum of the termination process becomes impossible to alter. Events become interpreted in such a way as to justify what is inevitably a difficult decision. The question is whether there is still reason to hope that you can change your fate.

If you believe that there is no turning back, then you can bet that it will be irreversible. The converse is not necessarily true. Just because you believe that you are right and can prove your worth does not make it so. This reaction may be sparked more by pride and ego than reality. The issue isn't whether you are good enough; it is whether the boss is convinced that your virtues outweigh any concerns about keeping you around. You should be objective in considering whether you can excel in the job and change the boss's predisposition about your worth.

If your basic nature is at the root of the differences, then you can't—and shouldn't—expect that you can become someone you're not for the sake of this job. On the other hand, if the clash is traceable to differences in assumptions and knowledge of the facts, then there may be the hope, through your education or the boss's, that the differences can be reconciled.

"Oh good. All I've got to do is convince my boss that I'm right." There is no arguing with that truth, except we are talking about the reality of changing someone else's attitudes and beliefs. Your chances would obviously be a lot better, and more under your control, if you knew and understood why the manager believes what he does and what is getting in your way. Once you can see things from the manager's perspective, you may discover that it is not so difficult to accept his views.

In summary, you have to make the difficult assessment about how convinced the boss is that you've got to go and whether your differences are reconcilable. Look for signs of hope and defeat. Try to let the situation—not your feelings—tell the story.

Is Your Job Worth Saving?

The organizational process of rejecting a member can be a rough, frustrating, and emotionally painful battle. Even if you have the stamina to ride it through, it may not be worth it. The choice of staying or leaving is yours. When you stop to think about it, the reasons for your rejection may be the same reasons you should be choosing to leave. If your ideas, beliefs, style, and personality are not compatible with the boss, and/or the organization, what do you have to gain—other than some egotistical notion of beating the rap and showing them a thing or two?

Don't be thrown by fears about what is available in the world outside the company. This country has tremendous opportunities for capable people who lead with their strengths. Assuming the critical differences had been reconciled, will the current situation allow you to flourish and succeed? Decide what you want out of your career. If the current situation will not allow you to realize your full potential, why bother knocking your head against the wall?

If, after objectively and critically matching yourself against your boss's view of the job and organizational requirements, you still believe that it is to your advantage to gain acceptance as a valued player, go for it.

Open Communication Lines with Your Boss

If your relationship with the boss has deteriorated, there has undoubtedly been a breakdown in communication. Whether this breakdown was the cause or result of your problem is irrelevant—either way successful reconciliation requires an open channel of communication. Only through dialogue can you uncover any misunderstandings that may be at the root of the problem. It is understandably difficult to reach out to someone who has deemed you unworthy. However, unless you can gain some modicum of rapport with this person, your cause is lost. You can let nature take its course or step into the lion's den. In most cases, the boss would rather not put someone out of work. It is possible that the manager doesn't care about what he does to other people, but why not assume that the person would like to find a way to make things right. If you think and act constructively, you may be pleasantly surprised to find a favorable attitude reciprocated.

Once you have decided to confront your boss, you must determine the best way to get effective communication flowing. There are different ways of attacking blocked communication.

At one extreme is the most frontal approach of forcing all the cards on the table: "I understand you're thinking of firing me!" Although it can be done with more finesse, the object of the directness is to trigger a blunt discussion about why your job is in jeopardy and what can be done about it. Depending on the situation and the personalities, this may be a downright gutsy move. It may force a confrontation that provides the boss with an ideal opportunity to do the deed. On the other hand, if your boss is still undecided about your fate and would just as soon avoid firing you, this kind of heart-to-heart talk could break the spell of a tenuous relationship. On balance, it is a high risk move with the greatest potential for producing movement — for better or worse.

A more conservative approach calls for increasing the frequency with which the two of you talk about the business and your work. The intent is to make a determined effort to be sure that the boss is fully informed about what you are doing and thinking and to correct any erroneous impressions. It also provides the opportunity for you to understand better the boss's views and where your points of conflict lie.

The latter course of action is crucial if your relationship has seriously deteriorated to the point that you have been avoiding each other. The boss should at least have to deal with the facts of your work and not only impressions that may be unduly influenced by his temperament or expectations.

Do not try to sell your boss on how good you are — this is likely to turn him off and keep you on opposite sides of the fence. Attempts at self-aggrandizement are invariably transparent and are likely to succeed in getting the boss to back off from spending time with you. Instead, use the opportunity to seek his counsel on how you could be more effective. You want to break down the sense that you are antagonists. Let your rapport rebuild itself naturally, allowing the boss the opportunity to discover that you can work together to resolve any conflicts. If the two of you can start talking about your performance, ideas, style, or whatever else is relevant to your status, then you may have sparked a hope for reconciliation.

Are You Correctly Interpreting
Each Other's Words?

Once you start talking to each other, make sure you are speaking the same language. Your manager's words may have a different meaning to her than they do to you and vice versa. This becomes particularly critical when the words are referring to constructs that are fundamental to how the individual sees or construes the world.

For example, to one manager, the dollar and cents return on investment may be the most highly valued measure of success or failure; for another it may be the size of the empire as measured by sales volume. So when the manager turns to you and demands action and results, make sure you know which yardstick is being used to measure success.

When the manager expresses a view of the business or of your efforts, listen carefully for the constructs that are continually and consistently used to distinguish between good and bad, success and failure, winning and losing, valuable and unimportant. Then make sure you understand what is meant by those critical constructs and why they are so important to the manager. Ask for clarification of the concepts that seem to drive your manager's attention and let her help you understand her views. You may find that you have been misinterpreting the words and inadvertently going against ideas that are central to your boss's thinking. You may not reconcile all your differences, but if you can at least be sure you're speaking the same language, you have a far better basis for repairing the relationship.

If you can't understand your boss's reaction to your

words or ideas, then you need to have your boss explain exactly what is causing the dissatisfaction. Be sure you are deciphering this person's messages carefully. This ultimately means finding out the constructs, words, or concepts that your boss uses in her own mind to draw the dividing line between what is highly valued and what is unacceptable.

Is the Channel of Communication Beyond Repair?

Your manager may already have a strong negative attitude toward you and anything you do. In that event, when you go searching for this person's critical values, you may discover to your dismay that the one construct that clearly and consistently differentiates his negative from his positive reactions is "you!" Your manager may even be indifferent to actions of yours that would have yielded praise if done by someone else. If such a negative image has started to take shape about you, then you have terrible static in your communication lines. This negative predisposition can keep you from ever getting into constructive dialogue. Bumping into such a wall is discouraging, distasteful, and futile — but you must know about it and face the reality of it.

In all likelihood, the manager's negative view of you originated with the belief or feeling that you clash with values that are near and dear to him. These values may be embedded in your manager's concept of where and how the business should go or, at a more personal level, the kinds of people your manager wants to be working with. The only avenue of hope is to figure out some way of showing your manager that you can help him realize his vision of success. If you can't find a way to eliminate or at least reduce this negative predisposition, you may have already passed the point of no return.

Reconcile Your Differences—Perhaps

If you are talking to each other and have taken out some of the interference in the line, you can work on reconciling your differences or at least working out some accommodation short of your leaving the organization. If the critical differences are ideas about what is best for the business, the gap may be one of information and knowledge—one knows something that the other doesn't. In that case, the open lines of communication can provide the opportunity for each of you to get up to speed with what the other knows.

If the clash is caused by differences in personality or style, the path to resolution is less evident and more difficult. Is one of you going to change how you naturally respond to situations? Should you try to become someone you're not? However, you could attempt to gain a better mutual understanding of why you don't see things eye to eye. Given your respective styles, why might each of you be disturbed by how the other person does things? If the two of you can acknowledge and discuss the differences in your styles, this would at least be a starting point to gaining some accommodation.

Aside from the issue of being fired, it is healthier—both mentally and organizationally—to face up to differences and at least gain an understanding of each other's point of view. Just because you don't have arguments over any differences doesn't mean that they are not there or that the boss is not contemplating a solution to resolving them. Though full agreement might not be achieved, there might be at least acceptance and respect for divergent points of view.

Reconciliation is a two-way street and not simply a matter of getting your manager to recognize that you're right and she is wrong. It's possible, but the odds are not in your favor. People's beliefs and attitudes gain a certain momentum — a body in motion tends to stay in motion. It can take an inordinate amount of evidence, proof, and persuasion to reverse a mind that is made up. This is especially true if others in the organization are reinforcing your boss's point of view and if your credibility has already begun to diminish.

You, on the other hand, have a clear incentive to change. Therefore, when you get to the point of openly discussing your disagreement, you might be better off focusing on understanding the manager's point of view. Be sure you are listening carefully to the manager and genuinely trying to see things from her perspective. Your manager has had different experiences and her position gives her a different perspective and exposure to other considerations. You always retain the right to find the manager's views unacceptable and to then pursue appropriate alternatives accordingly.

Ultimately, you may find that it just can't work. Be prepared for that moment of truth — and remember this does not make you a failure. If you don't fit in, even after years of having been an integral part of an organization, it is not a reflection of your worth but the fate of circumstances.

Don't Let the Loser Syndrome Defeat You

As you attempt to regain your foothold within the company there is a mind set that may be fighting against your efforts: the loser syndrome. You must be alert to it or you could be defeated before you have had a fair chance to fight back.

Picture being in a situation in which the boss has lost confidence in you and expects you to fail. Worse yet, the people around you pick up on the boss's attitude, perhaps even finding it advantageous to confirm the negative expectations. If that's not enough, envision being a lame duck with your subordinates. The smell of defeat in the orgainzation finds its way into your pores. You begin to feel powerless and defeated. You question your own capability and adopt your manager's doubts about you.

The conspiracy of all these events is the loser syndrome. Guard against it. You can't afford to let yourself be dragged down by the weight of such a burden or you will lose the objectivity and clarity of vision that is needed to see your way through this difficult time. Watch for signs of negative expectations and keep them from becoming self-fulfilling prophecies.

Seek an Influential Ally

So far you have been going it alone. You need allies. Friends you can trust are always important for support, comfort, and advice. A supporter who has the ear of the boss can be invaluable if the person is willing to serve as a go-between, a conciliator, a counsel to the court. Even someone with a neutral posture about your predicament, such as a human resource professional, can help both sides of the conflict see the situation more clearly.

The best ally is a mentor who cares about preventing the loss of a valuable employee and has been privy to the boss's thoughts about you and the organization. It is important that the mentor know you well enough to understand how you match up against what the boss needs, why the problem has erupted, and how it can be straightened out. After looking into the problem the mentor may agree with your boss's view, but even then the mentor may be more willing than your boss to lay the cards on the table. It is better to know the harsh reality of what you are up against.

Even allies that are not so well placed can help you see more clearly what is happening to you. You just have to be careful about relying on the opinions of someone who, unbeknownst to you, may be in the same predicament. Such a person might mirror and perhaps erroneously validate what you believe. This can have the opposite effect of a good mentor and reinforce maladaptive responses.

If you go about finding a mentor in a constructive manner, you just may find someone who can help you to get back in command. Even if you end up being terminated, at least you will have a clearer understanding of what happened to you.

Line up Your Alternatives

At any point along the way, it is not too early to get the wheels in motion for finding another job. Actively job hunting while trying to salvage the one you are in can be an onerous, if not schizophrenic, task. However, it is not unreasonable to start thinking about the steps that would be appropriate to land another job.

Set aside some time, preferably on weekends, when you can get some distance from the pressures of the on-going dilemma and do some preliminary thinking about job hunting. You don't have to be out of work to learn how to market yourself effectively. It can be helpful to read one of the books available on how to conduct a job search.

As you think about the pursuit of alternative opportunities, you may even gain insight for reexamining your current situation while there is still time to do something about it. Reflecting on your strengths and weaknesses and how you would position your experience and capabilities with a new employer is a constructive exercise and important in keeping a perspective on your situation. How far you get into an active search posture would depend on how convinced you are that you have passed the point of no return and whether such an effort would put your current situation further in jeopardy.

At a minimum, you should be building contacts that can be helpful if and when you undertake a full-scale job search. Renew acquaintances with people you know and see who can introduce you to other people. You never know who will be able to lead you to the job you may one day seek to find. Building and maintaining contacts outside your organization can also help you keep current and protect against conceptual obsolescence. Furthermore, an outside vantage point may help you see and understand more clearly what has been happening to you in your own organization. One of these outsiders may help you learn more about the boss and why the two of you are having trouble. There are no advantages to being insulated within your own organization.

NEXT TIME—SUCCEEDING WITH A NEW BOSS

Reversing a situation that has gone bad is a difficult struggle. It is never too soon to consider your compatibility with a boss. This is especially appropriate when you are about to go to work for a new boss.

Before You Accept That Next Job

All too often people do an abysmal job of evaluating a prospective employer. Typically, a job candidate will look at the job, the company's prospects, and surface impressions of management. Few ask searching and critical questions to uncover why they shouldn't want what appears to be an inviting opportunity. It is too easy—and tempting—to shift prematurely from "Why should I take this job?" to "I hope I get it." When you get sold on the job, you stop looking for why the fit may not be good.

To a large extent, the prospective employer controls the interview process. However, an interview should be a two-way assessment. Use it.

Be assertive in asking questions or resolving doubts.

Keep a sharp eye on the distinction between what you know and how you assume things will be.

Seek clarification of broad generalizations and especially any inconsistencies.

Reconfirm your understanding of what is expected from you, including the nature of the role you are expected to fulfill.

Be sure there is at least one informal, relaxed meeting, perhaps over lunch or dinner, for you and your future boss to test the personal side of the fit.

It is easy to be lulled into believing that this marriage was made in corporate heaven. However, you must be sure that you are speaking the same language. There is nothing wrong with being enthusiastic or excited about a great opportunity. But go forward with both eyes wide open.

You have no reason to hold back on asking tough questions. As a matter of fact, most employers are impressed by someone who asks tough questions and doesn't hesitate to find out what they want to know. It is a sign of strength, not weakness, to be smart about where you are going.

Try to get to know the other key players in the organization, especially your boss's manager and the people who would be your peers. This gives you a chance to test your fit with the organization and not just the boss. The boss may not be representative of the prevailing values and thinking. Don't be reluctant to ask any of these other people for their view of the business, how the organization functions, what is expected of you, and even what the boss is like.

Master the New Culture

When you enter a new organization or a new part of the same company, it is best to assume that every organization has some values, beliefs, or rules that make it different from whatever you have been accustomed to. Be alert for the differences and how your usual way of doing things might clash with the existing norms and patterns. This does not mean that you should not attempt to invoke change—but it is important to know where you are starting from.

People will naturally adapt to each other or eventually break apart. Instead of just letting nature take its course, try to facilitate your assimilation. Make an effort to help people understand your points of view and why you may see things differently. In the same vein, listen to them and attempt to reconcile differences before they become an obstacle to your acceptance. If you attempt to fight against the basic beliefs or values of the organization, with neither side making an accommodation, you may be moving closer to your eventual extrication by the organization.

Building a Relationship with a New Boss

The best way of keeping a relationship from going haywire for the wrong reasons is to have open communication right from the start. Keep your boss well informed at all times. Make sure you both have a common understanding of each other's expectations about the opportunities, obstacles, expected results, and ground rules regarding the functioning of the organization and your role.

When you sense conflict, get it out into the open without giving it a chance to fester, distort perceptions, and become irreversible. Enter into dialogue with the manager when the two of you can informally explore your respective ideas about the business and what success or failure means to each of you. Brief, formal meetings that focus on targets and results are important, but they are not substitutes for really getting to understand each other's ideas, values, perspectives, and idiosyncrasies. These are the areas where differences are more likely to cause problems—and the areas hardest to reconcile after the relationship has deteriorated.

Gaining a mutual understanding and respect for each other is not the same thing as playing up to the boss and telling him whatever he wants to hear. In one case, you are an individual with a mind of your own, seeking to build a constructive, healthy, working relationship. In the other instance, you are acting out of fear and from a position of weakness. In the long run, the latter affords you no protection against failure while the former at least gives you self-respect and a position of strength for recovering from a stumble.

Develop Your Outside Contacts

The importance of keeping in touch with people outside your organization was mentioned earlier. Even though you have started a new job, friends and associates from other organizations can provide valuable perspectives as you seek to understanding your new boss and attempt to reconcile your differences. Besides, the best time to build a safety net is when you don't need it. It takes time to establish relationships—it is too late to fill the water buckets when the house is burning down!

Chapter Eight

A Guide for the Boss

How to Avoid Firing Good People

The preceding chapters of this book were written to help the individual rise above a clash with a boss. This chapter talks to the boss — whether a supervisor of a few employees or the chief executive responsible for thousands — who wants to know what can be done to avoid the wasteful firing of talented managers. It should also be of interest to the human resource professional charged with helping the boss meet this challenge.

Your task is to evaluate your own particular organization and determine the steps that would be most appropriate. Following a consultative posture, various questions will serve to guide you through this self-analysis.

ARE TALENTED PEOPLE BEING FIRED IN YOUR ORGANIZATION?

Before undertaking a study of your entire organization, think back over the recent past to any subordinates who had been fired by you or by the managers who report to you.

How long had the terminated individuals been working for you or the boss who fired them? Did the terminations involve new boss–subordinate relationships?

Were the failures related to a bad fit between the terminated subordinate and a new boss?

Were capable new hires unable to adapt to your way of doing things?

Were they incompatible with the values and attitudes of the organization?

Were they dedicated people with years of experience in your organization?

Did the terminees have valuable knowledge and skills?

If this preliminary glimpse has stimulated your concern, or at least piqued your curiosity, look for indications of these problems deeper in the organization. To do this you need turnover statistics that will tell you how long terminees had been working for the boss who fired them. More often than not, firings related to a new boss–subordinate relationship are caused by a difficult fit rather than inadequate capability. The following information would be useful for diagnosing bad termination trends.

What proportion of the terminees were fired within a year or two of working for a new boss?

If the "new boss" phenomenon is evident, what proportion of the terminees were newly hired, recently promoted, or subordinates under a newly appointed manager?

What is the organization's track record in absorbing new employees?

Do new hires tend to clean house? Does this phenomenon cascade down through succeeding levels of the organization?

Is the tenure of employees getting shorter?

Look for organizational pockets that suffer high loss rates. Heads of self-contained units, such as divisions, plants, or geographic regions, often develop a strong sense of ownership and the righteous feeling that things should be done their way. These situations have the greatest potential for triggering the domino effect — the cascading of one level of managers replacing the next with replacements who are more in keeping with the new wave.

> Is there a substantial replacement of people after someone is put in charge of one of these independent units?
>
> Are the new breeds left without the benefit of the experience and knowledge of the seasoned employees who could no longer fit in?
>
> How long does it take for the newcomers to learn the business and mesh into a unified and effectively functioning organizational machine?
>
> Is the restaffed organization competitively stronger or weaker?

As the result of a merger or acquisition, you may be presiding over a major addition to your organization. Corporate takeovers usually result in the loss of the very talent that probably made the business worth acquiring in the first place. It is often culture clash on a grand scale, with the acquiring organization being "the new boss" over many subordinates struggling to fit in. If there has been a recent takeover, check for talent drain. Eliminating redundancy is one thing; replacing valuable managers is another.

In examining termination trends, an important consideration is certainly whether the organization is better off without the people who have been fired. This is hard to determine especially since the dynamics of terminations invariably casts a dark shadow on the capabilities of those asked to leave. You will have to judge whether the pattern revealed by the numbers is acceptable and if you want to do something about it.

BETTER INPLACEMENT MEANS LESS OUTPLACEMENT

A major premise of this book is that fatal clashes between bosses and subordinates are most likely to occur when a new person is brought into an organization. Therefore the guiding principle for the avoidance of wasteful terminations is: Better inplacement will reduce outplacement. Managers should take constructive action at the following critical junctures of a new employee's entry:

Before Entry. Determine the personal attributes that will result in a good or bad fit with the boss and with the organization.

Selection. Assess the total person against the organizational considerations.

Negotiation. Before hiring the candidate, make sure that there is a mutual understanding of the job and expectations about role and performance.

Entry. Take an active role in facilitating the new person's assimilation into the organization.

Six Months Later. Reevaluate the new person and his subordinates; plan developmental actions for dealing with termination risks.

The focus is on prevention, rather than the resolution of fatal clashes that have deteriorated past the point of no return. After a boss–subordinate relationship has thundered into a downward cycle of adversity, it is usually too late to reverse the countdown. The investment of time and effort during the early stages of inplacement is the most practical approach. The following actions can increase the likelihood of successful inplacement. Be prepared, in the privacy of your reading chair, to challenge whether you actually do as much as you might to help your subordinates be succcessful.

Before Entry— Measuring the Fit

When considering the requirements of a job, the technical aspects are usually spelled out. People are rarely fired for a shortfall in technical knowledge or skill. However, personality and organizational relationships can prevent managers from effectively utilizing their valuable experience. Therefore, it is important to look beyond the technical requirements and to give due consideration to the organizational context of the job.

MATCHING THE BOSS. Assuming that you are the boss, are certain types of people more or less likely to succeed or fail when working for you? This requires an honest, objective self-analysis.

What is your dominant style of working, thinking, deciding, and leading?

Are you a forceful driver or a friendly diplomat? An objective analyst or an enthusiastic persuader?

Do you work effectively with people who have a particular style or temperament?

Will certain characteristics doom a subordinate's chance of survival?

What makes the smooth relationships smooth?

Why are some people a natural fit and others not?

Do you consider certain management philosophies or strategies to be sacrosanct?

How do you expect people to fit in with your efforts?

Are you invariably surrounded by a wide diversity of personality types or do you prefer people cut from a particular cloth?

What is your tolerance for divergent points of view?

Whether you choose to openly talk about your tolerance and acceptance of various types of people, at least know in your own mind (and heart) what it takes to be successful working for you.

MATCHING THE ORGANIZATION. The organization's culture — beliefs, values, attitudes — should also be considered. For example, someone with a bureaucratic bent is likely to have trouble in an unstructured, free-wheeling environment. As the boss, you should ask yourself the following questions:

Are certain types of people not going to fit in?

Were those who have not done well in this organization different from most insiders? If so, how?

Is a certain management style likely to be ineffective with the people who will be working for the new employee?

MATCHING THE STRATEGY. Ultimately, the most critical consideration in picking new people should be the strategy of the organization. It is vital that any key person have qualities that can give the business a strategic advantage over your competitors. Competitive analysis, a technique used to develop business strategy, can be useful in determining how employees can increase a business's competitive edge. The following questions about strategy should be asked:

Do you have definite ideas about the strategic thrust of the organization?

How do you intend to outdo the competition?

How do you expect the new person to impact the execution of the competitive strategy?

What type of person is most likely to succeed in pursuing the strategy?

What personal characteristics are likely to run counter to the strategic direction?

INSERTING A MISMATCH TO CAUSE CHANGE. If the culture of the organization is well suited to the competitive strategy, then certain types of individuals are likely to be a good fit for both the strategy and the organization. However, in this ever-changing world, you may be pursuing a strategic direction that is a drastic departure for the organization. If the entrenched culture is poorly matched to the new thrust, you may decide to insert someone who fits the strategy but not the organization.

Thoughtful attention to inplacement is especially critical when you inject such an agent of change. Organizations tend to put pressure on getting misfits expelled. Depending on the balance of power, those clinging to old ways may be the casualties. Assimilating a mismatch is not an easy chore. The time to give it your best effort is before you do it — not afterwards when you have to go around picking up the pieces.

The Selection Decision — Assessing the Total Person

It is relatively easy to size up a candidate's technical capability. As mentioned before, this is rarely the reason for a bad hire. The hard part is assessing the human side of a person — gaining a clear picture of temperament, style, values, and attitudes. In the world of management, these are the traits that underlie success or failure.

Unfortunately, it is exceedingly difficult to get to know the human side of a candidate. It is natural for people to try to present themselves in the most favorable light possible. The pressure and tension of being evaluated invariably result in guardedness. Aside from specific assessment techniques, you need to spend enough time, in a range of situations, until the guard is lowered. A one-hour interview barely scratches the surface and should be considered only a first step—though an important one.

Your initial face-to-face encounter with a candidate can be a revealing microcosm of how the future relationship between the two of you is likely to unfold. Depending on each person's personality, each one will bring out certain reactions from the other. Take note of your own reactions throughout the screening process: They are important clues to what direction the relationship will take. For example, if you are more directive than usual in keeping the interview conversation moving forward, this may foreshadow a subordinate who will require close guidance from you.

Be attentive to your negative reactions, even if you're not sure what is bothering you: They may be telling clues to a serious incompatibility. Too often managers shrug off seemingly minor and irrelevant reactions, only to discover, in the midst of a deteriorating relationship, what the warning meant.

If the outcome of the initial interview is positive, it should be followed by other meetings. Look for situations that will help the person relax and allow his natural style and manner to emerge—perhaps an informal dinner, a visit to one of your facilities, or even someplace on the candidate's home ground. A meeting at the person's office—which is not as out of the question as you may think—can be revealing.

Until you have a reasonably good fix on the candidate, keep the assessment process alive. If you don't think you can learn any more from additional interviews, have another person join the two of you. While they are getting to know each other, you can sit back and be an attentive observer. You may notice reactions that were not evident when you were busily engaged in the give and take of conversation. Also, interviews conducted by other people can provide different perspectives and help to test your perceptions.

When you have constructed a consistent picture of the total person, match the characteristics against the organizational requirements. Any placement decision is invariably a compromise—it is unrealistic to expect to find a perfect fit. At least you can go forward with realistic expectations, taking your concerns into consideration when trying to help the person be successful.

The Offer—Closing the Deal

You have decided that the candidate is right for the job and are about to extend the offer. Discussions of the conditions of employment are usually limited to the details of the financial package. This is also the time to be sure that your respective assumptions and expectations about the job are consistent and compatible.

It is especially important to cover the areas that are often the cause of problems in a placement: differences over strategy, management philosophy, and the person's role in the organization. Also be sure you see eye to eye on what is to be accomplished and how, including how you intend to measure success or failure. Do not make the common mistake of assuming that these matters are self-evident or will somehow work themselves out afterward.

Entry—Managing Assimilation

The person's entry into your organization is critical. Every organization has its own way of doing things. Misunderstandings easily arise when people follow patterns that were previously successful, but unknowingly clash with the unspoken rules and norms of the new organization. Words and actions can take on different meanings, with misinterpretations leading to misunderstandings. You should play an active role in helping your new subordinate become assimilated within the organization—to accelerate the newcomer's mastery of the situation, forestall misunderstandings, and minimize counterproductive conflict.

ORIENTING THE NEWCOMER. In planning the new employee's entry, identify the people who will be critical to his success. This includes your other subordinates, the staff who will be working for the new person, and anyone else whose responsibilities impact the person's job. The following questions will help prepare an orientation plan.

Do these critical people know what you expect from the new person?

Do they understand your intentions and the support you want from them?

Do any particular roles and relationships warrant additional clarification?

Can you anticipate any resistance to the newcomer's entry?

Are there fears or resentment that should be dealt with beforehand?

What can be done during the initial months to accelerate the entrant's mastery of the business?

Are there plans or reports the new person should read, places to visit, outsiders to meet?

Who should seek out the new hire upon arrival to help build a constructive relationship?

Can someone, perhaps from the human resources staff, serve as a third-party facilitator to help the new employee make this transition and bridge communication problems in any of the important relationships—including the one with you.

Depending on your style, putting an orientation plan in writing may seem excessive, but it is too easy to assume that these early steps will happen and take care of themselves. The plan may be no more than a schedule of the people to meet, places to visit, and things to read—but it forces you to give prior thought to the inplacement. A concrete plan alerts the organization and the newcomer that you expect the assimilation to be treated as a serious, purposeful, and active process.

BUILDING YOUR RELATIONSHIP. When the new person arrives, the most important thing you can do is to build an open channel of communication. This is the best antidote to keeping the inplacement from going awry. You want to know if and when the assimilation is being bogged down by conflict so that you can do something about it before it becomes a difficult problem. In short, take advantage of your mutual respect before those feelings become dissipated.

Set a tone to the relationship so that the new person will be open to express any concerns and accept your help.

Tell the new person what you expect and how you will measure successful performance.

Clearly explain your ideas about the direction of the business, the functioning of the organization, and your respective roles.

Give the new person constructive feedback about how he is adjusting and mastering the situation.

It is a good idea to mark your own calender for periodic chats with the new employee. Some of these discussions should be informal and take place out of the office, perhaps over lunch or dinner. It is too easy to let the months slip by without taking the time to help the new person work out any difficulties in the assimilation. When the situation gets out of hand, it does no good to wish you had made more of an effort along the way.

The Six Month Review

By six months into the job, the new person has formed impressions of any inherited subordinates. This is an appropriate time to discuss these views, especially since it is probably evident by now if any of these subordinates are on the road to termination. You should also take a hard look at the new person to consider if the placement is proving to be successful.

EVALUATING THE SUBORDINATE. Have the person prepare a one-page written assessment of his subordinates, highlighting strengths and problems. The discipline of writing the assessment, though admittedly a demanding chore, is worth the effort. It forces the new manager to pause, step back, and think about his impressions and reactions, thus fostering objectivity in considering the issues of capability and fit.

A useful approach for constructing these evaluations is the conjoint assessment technique. This involves having a qualified human resource professional work with a manager on preparing the assessments. The professional interviews the manager about each subordinate and drafts the reports. Then they work together on refining the assessment, with the manager making sure that the final report accurately reflects his view of the person. In effect, they will have "conjointly" constructed the assessments, utilizing the manager's knowledge and the professional's objectivity and assessment skills. This technique can be used by you in assessing the new employee and by him in assessing any of his subordinates.

After the assessments are completed, by whatever technique, you should conduct a management review meeting with the new person. This should be an informal, private session in which the new person can feel comfortable about revealing his impressions, reactions, and conclusions. You want an open give-and-take discussion on sensitive questions. Overly formal presentations, with too many interested parties sitting around a table, easily gravitate toward superficial conversation. However, it can be useful to include a trusted and respected human resource professional who has been working closely with both of you on the inplacement.

An appropriate starting point is a brief review of the organization's objectives and strategy. Then the new manager should tell you about each subordinate's performance, capability, style, and fit. The new manager's reactions to how the subordinates match or complement his own style should also be explored, especially if there is discomfort about any particular fit. Review any plans to change the organization—be it the culture or the people. This is a good opportunity for you to help resolve any conflicts or find solutions to a problematic misfit. At the end of the session, seek agreement to any organizational issues and areas warranting follow-up action.

PLANNING DEVELOPMENTAL ACTIONS. The new manager should prepare an action plan for any subordinate who is having difficulty. The development plan should start with a succinct statement about what is impeding success, including any problems in adapting to the changes brought on by the new manager.

The crucial part of the development plan is a list of concrete actions to be taken to overcome the difficulties. A timetable for executing each step of the plan should be included so that you can readily monitor progress. The new manager should review the development plan with each subordinate, letting it serve as a constructive vehicle for them to work out any problems.

In the event that the new manager wants to terminate any of the subordinates, you have to decide whether you are prepared to keep your money riding on this person before he starts to undo the organization. The last thing you need is the replacement of the subordinates followed by a dethroning of their leader.

If the new person doesn't fit the business, the culture, or you — there is a better than even chance that the replacements he brings in won't either. The compounding effect of a mistake can be catastrophic. You should address any issues concerning this person now before events take over and rob you of your choices.

EVALUATING THE NEW EMPLOYEE. To complete the total picture, you need to assess the new person. Write down your conclusions about the person's performance, capability, style, and fit. Then consider the following:

How well does the person match the strategy?

Is the person providing the competitive edge you had hoped for?

Does the person function effectively in the organization?

Have the two of you developed a constructive working relationship?

Are there any significant shortcomings or differences that, unless reconciled, will be a significant detriment to accomplishing your objectives?

Do you have the right person in the job?

What can you do to help the person be more successful?

After completing the assessment, prepare a developmental action plan. Then sit down with the person to discuss your impressions, concerns, and ideas on how he could be more effective. If you have held back on telling the person anything that troubles you about your relationship or his functioning within the organization, now is the time to get it out on the table. Take the person through the development plan and be sure he understands what is expected and what you intend to do to help. Set a date for a follow-up meeting to review progress in implementing the plan.

This is all good and well if there are minor shortcomings or reconcilable differences, but what if the situation is on the verge of failure? If there is any hope of it being corrected, the person should be told about your concerns and the magnitude of the problem. It is extremely difficult to tell someone that his job is on the line and what must be done to save it. However, it is usually the only way to help turn it around. If you want to give the person a chance, now is the time to attempt a satisfactory reconciliation. A third party may be able to help the two of you to overcome miscommunication or misunderstandings.

After doing all you can to make it work, it may become evident that it is a bad fit that can't be fixed. The gap may be too wide or there may be too much resistance. It may be time to cut your losses before the wrong person has a detrimental impact on the organization.

In implementing an active inplacement process at various levels of your organization, certain factors will determine its effectiveness. The remainder of this chapter focuses on these factors and what you can do to foster a successful effort.

DO THE VALUES AND BELIEFS OF YOUR ORGANIZATION PROMOTE THE RESOLUTION OF PROBLEMS OF ENTRY AND FIT?

Certain attitudes in American society virtually discourage people from taking some inplacement actions that could prevent unnecessary firings. Are these attitudes prevalent in your organization?

Individual Responsiblity. Each individual is responsible for his own actions. If anyone fails, he has only himself to blame.

Self-Reliance. It is a sign of weakness to admit to defeat or to seek help from a manager. The boss is not expected to coddle subordinates who are being paid good money to get the job done.

Subordination. Employees are paid to meet the boss's standards and expectations. It is for the subordinate to adapt to the boss and not vice versa.

Tolerance. A manager is expected to get results and should not tolerate shortcomings or mistakes. If there is a failure, the strong boss acts decisively in replacing the person who failed.

Don't be too quick to conclude which attitudes prevail in your organization. Building a culture that is conducive to the utilization of existing talent and forestalling fatal relationship problems must start with leadership from the top down. At a minimum, you need to raise a red flag; let it be known that you do not want to lose talented people because they are having trouble fitting in with a boss. The organization needs to find out that you want both bosses and subordinates to take an active and constructive role in resolving their differences.

Leadership

The most powerful influence is the example you set. Over time, it is the leader's actions, not his or her words, that shape the culture. When a leader fires someone, the organization scrambles to find out what happened. They want to know your ground rules for getting fired. Unfortunately, people rarely realize or appreciate how much thought, effort, and perhaps even agony have gone into your decision to terminate someone. Human nature being what it is, a boss rarely is given the benefit of the doubt when someone is fired.

It is easier to communicate your attitudes when someone else is firing a subordinate. Your reactions and the questions you ask send strong signals that are more potent than policies or speeches.

Do you push to understand why the employee must be let go?

Do you explore the relationship between the subordinate and the boss, seeking to discover if every reasonable effort was made to reconcile their differences?

Do you make sure that the boss did enough to help the person succeed?

Do you see if a reasonable attempt was made to find an opportunity to utilize the employee's talents elsewhere in the organization?

Management Reviews

A formal process of reviewing managers can be an ideal mechanism for institutionalizing the key elements of effective inplacement. If conducted on a regular basis, the reviews would flag the need for intervention while there is still hope of averting a wasteful termination. The reviews can alert you to the expected entry of new employees, thus providing the opportunity to ensure that appropriate attention is given to assimilation. It is also a natural vehicle for closely tracking the progress of both new placements and their subordinates during the critical early stages of entry. In effect, the "six month review" of a new employee would be done within the structure of the normal management review process.

When a new entrant is planning staffing changes, your review should be particularly thorough. You want to understand how the person sees people and whether you are comfortable with the basis on wh'˜h anyone is being replaced. This opens the door to a dialogue on your respective views about balancing the utilization of existing talent and the need for new blood. Finally, the process can easily end up being a meaningless paper exercise if there isn't active follow-up to ensure that development plans are converted into real action.

Termination Tracking

Another way to get an organization to focus attention on the issue of wasteful terminations is to measure and closely monitor trends. Turnover figures should include the measures mentioned earlier, such as how many people are terminated after the entry of someone new.

These measures are a means of uncovering trouble spots, such as specific units with an influx of new managers driving out seasoned employees. Where trouble is brewing, top to bottom management reviews should be conducted to understand the cause and get it remedied. If people realize that management is watching these trends, they are more likely to try harder to keep from losing good talent.

Policies

A company's policies should reinforce the institutionalization of constructive inplacement actions, including safeguards to ensure that appropriate steps are taken before someone is terminated. However, this written code of behavior cannot take the place of visible leadership — prevailing attitudes find a way around the rules.

ARE THIRD-PARTY FACILITATORS AVAILABLE TO HELP PEOPLE CAUGHT IN A CLASH?

When a relationship is deteriorating, a third party who is known and trusted by both parties can often calm the waters. In a formal mentor program, senior managers are assigned the task of providing support and guidance to people in the organization. Unfortunately, not all executives are inclined to be counselors, especially if they have to mediate a sticky conflict. With or without a formal program, the concept of helping others succeed should be fostered.

A clear message should be sent to the organization that upper-level people are expected to be available to provide advice and counsel. As the leader, you need to set the example and openly give recognition to the executives who provide effective mentoring. Employees should be encouraged to seek out and build informal relationships with the more experienced managers. An open door policy is essential to legitimize what might otherwise be seen as "going around the boss"; subordinates locked into the chain of command have no escape route to avoid a fatal clash.

A human resource professional who is seen as being a trusted and respected member of management can serve an important role. It takes time, as well as skill, to become established in this capacity, especially since people may be reluctant to expose their difficulties to someone in senior management.

Either the mentor or the staff professional can serve the multifaceted role of third party facilitator. Such a facilitator can help managers retain objectivity and perspective in their view of subordinates, especially to help keep bad relationships from clouding the issue of performance and capability.

The facilitator can bridge a bad communication gap between the boss and subordinate, helping them both to see more clearly their differences and find a way to gain accommodation. Also, the facilitator can bring other resources into play, such as the manager of the boss or an outside professional counselor. If the situation is irreparable, the facilitator may be in a good position to help the subordinate chart an alternative course in a positive, rather than defeatist, frame of mind.

DO EMPLOYEES HAVE THE OPPORTUNITY TO FIND A BETTER FIT ELSEWHERE IN THE COMPANY?

The facilitator, or someone else within personnel, can help to find other opportunities within the company to take advantage of the person's abilities and knowledge. The individual handling the internal placement must be trusted as an honest broker, and have credibility in sizing up people. The search for a better fitting opportunity needs to get underway before the prospect's reputation in the organization is tarnished beyond repair. Also, if the staff is involved early in the conflict, the parties involved are more likely to be objective in their views of the person and how he could be utilized in a different department. With a more accurate picture of the person's capability and style, the placement staff would be more effective in representing the candidate and salvaging the talent for the organization.

ARE MANAGERS SKILLED IN THE BASICS OF MANAGEMENT ASSESSMENT AND PERFORMANCE COUNSELING?

Managers, be they in the role of subordinate or boss, would be more effective in dealing with clashes over incompatibility if they had a better understanding of how stylistic differences can undermine relationships. A worthy objective of management training would be to develop leaders who can more effectively manage a diversity of people and take advantage of talent—even if it is cut from a different cloth.

Starting with candidate selection, management training could help to develop assessment skills. Managers should develop the ability to recognize the early signs of incompatibility, accept interpersonal differences for what they are, and find ways to gain accommodation. Appropriate training would give managers insight into their reactions to different types of people, as well as the reactions of other people to them. Accommodation and reconciliation between clashing individuals is more likely if they can see the world through each other's eyes.

Both bosses and subordinates could be shown how to be more effective in keeping channels of communication open, especially to facilitate the feedback that is needed for people to adapt to each other. There are often programs for teaching managers how to give feedback to subordinates; little attention is paid to showing subordinates how to serve an active and constructive role in getting the boss to tell them how they can be more effective.

ARE MANAGERS ALLOWED TO BECOME CONCEPTUALLY OBSOLETE

When someone stays in the same job and in the same company for a long time, they are prone to becoming obsolete in their thinking. Aside from being a problem in its own right, this significantly increases the risk of a terminal clash when a new boss with fresh perspectives is introduced into the organization. The following are a few suggestions for keeping insiders as current as outsiders.

Tack the tenure of employees to find out if anyone is stuck in the same job too long. Consider the advisability of job rotation or special assignments to give such managers a fresh outlook.

Encourage people to take time to expose their minds to current trends and thinking by reading, attending seminars, or building relationships with their peers in other companies.

Require managers to spend time with employees in the field, as well as customers and suppliers. Encourage them to establish relationships with people from diverse corners of the organization.

Encourage people to venture outside their functional specialty—this is the food of innovation and creativity.

DOES THE ORGANIZATION HAVE THE VIBRANCY AND RESILIENCE TO ABSORB CHANGE?

The competitive world is changing at an accelerating rate, fueled by rapid technological advances, the information explosion, and an ever-shrinking globe. As society is impacted by these fast-paced changes, demands in the marketplace seem to shift overnight. To remain a strong competitor in this unpredictable world, a company must stay closely tuned in to the changes and be ready to take advantage of emerging opportunities.

An organization's capacity to remain a strong and viable competitor depends on its reservoir of talent. These people must keep pace with the myriad of changes and understand the implications for the business. They must be in synch with the emergent strategy if the company is to go forward with a superior competitive edge. In addition, their skills and temperament must be well matched to the strategy.

The challenge for leadership is to give an organization the capacity to effectively assimilate new ideas and new people without losing its valuable reservoir of experienced talent. The risk of termination increases when an organization radically changes its thinking. As new managers, in tune with the times are introduced into the mix, those who have fallen behind are likely to clash with the new breed. There is a good chance they won't understand each other's points of view and their differences will become translated into issues of incompetence. Thus, keeping an organization more vital — competitive — by helping its managers to keep pace with an ever-changing world is worth a sizable investment.

Diversity provides a breeding ground for new ideas and different perspectives for seeing the possibilities of the future. An organization with the resiliency to accept and assimilate a greater diversity of people has more flexibility for both coping with change and changing to meet the new shape of tomorrow's challenges.

References

Bolton, Robert, and Dorothy G. Bolton, *Social Style/Management Style*. New York: American Management Associations, 1984.

Brown, L. David, *Managing Conflict at Organizational Interfaces*. Reading, MA: Addison-Wesley, 1983.

Ewing, David W., *Do It My Way Or You're Fired!* New York: Wiley, 1983.

Gould, Richard, "Conjoint Executive Assessment for Strategic Planning," *Personnel Administrator* (April 1985): 51–56.

Keirsey, David, and Marilyn Bates, *Please Understand Me*. Del Mar, CA: Prometheus Nemesis, 1984.

Kelly, George A., *The Psychology of Personal Constructs*, vols. 1 and 2. New York: Norton, 1955.

Laing, R.D., *Knots*. New York: Pantheon Books, 1970.

Landfield, A.W., and L.M. Leitner, *Personal Construct Psychology*. New York: Wiley, 1980.

McCall, Jr., Morgan W., and Michael M. Lombardo, *Off the Track: Why and How Successful Executives Get Derailed*. Greensboro, NC: Center for Creative Leadership, 1983.

"Turnover at the Top," *Business Week*, December 19, 1983, 104–110.

Wanous, J.P., *Organizational Entry: Recruitment, Selection, and Socialization of Newcomers*. Reading, MA: Addison-Wesley, 1980.

INDEX

Index

Bitterness, 43
Blame:
  attribution of, 17, 35, 44
  struggle over, 32–34, 43, 44
Blunt, 73, 74, 75, 150
Boss, guide for, 166–191
Boss–subordinate relationship:
  deterioration, 16, 19, 36, 149
  discomfort, 34, 37
  signs of trouble, 140–142
Brassiness, 110
Breakdown in communication, see
  Communication
Brusqueness, 103
Bureaucratic philosophy, 52, 55, 96

Calm, 76
Capability and termination, 13–16
Career progress and termination, 2,
  127, 136
Cascading of firings, 98, 167–168
Case studies, see italicized entries
Cautiousness, 65
Cautious planner, 52, 54, 55
Center for Creative Leadership, 13
Change, adapting to, 180
Chief executive, 121–122
Clash, predictability of, 47
Cocoon, bounded, 90
Collision course, 21–44, 144
Communication:
  breakdown, 36, 38, 149–151
  bridging gap, 187
  channel, 150, 153, 177, 189
  faulty, 39, 82
  new relationship, 161
  reducing interference, 154
Compassion, 72, 74
Competitive:
  change, 93, 190
  edge, 191
  strategy, 79
  threat, 139
Competitiveness, 88, 113

Complacency, 67
Complementary relationship, 64,
  68, 75, 76, 129
Compulsive, 58
Conceptualizer, 60
Conceptual obsolescence, see
  Obsolescence, conceptual
Conciliator, see Third party,
  facilitator
Concrete thinker, 60
Confidence:
  undaunted, 71
  undermined, 7
Confining, 52
Conflict:
  resolution, 151, 162, 180, 184
  underlying cause, 142
Confrontation, 31, 32, 95, 150
Confusion surrounding termination,
  9, 16, 41
Congeniality, 4, 44, 73
Conjoint assessment, 179
Conspiracy of forces, 42
Constructive feedback, 32, 36, 178,
  189
Constructs, see Personal constructs
Contacts, building, 158, 162
Contemporary viewpoints, 89
Contradictions, 44
Control, organizational, 93, 97
Controlling style, 52, 53, 68, 113
Conviction, sense of, 99
Cooperative spirit, 107, 112
Corporate takeovers, 137, 168
Cost cutting, 83
Counselor, 54, 59, 82, 186–188
Credibility, 50, 155
Criticism, 110
Culture:
  and assimilation, 183–184
  change, 88, 92, 93, 173
  clash, 168
  corporate, 26, 102, 105, 138
  new, 161

Index

Index

DATE DUE

APR